ANATOMY
AND
REFLEXOLOGY
HELPER AREAS

STUDY GUIDE

by
Dwight C. Byers and Nancy S. Byers

INGHAM PUBLISHING, INC. - PUBLISHER
St. Petersburg, Florida, U.S.A.

Published and Distributed Throughout the World by

INGHAM PUBLISHING, INC. - PUBLISHER
Post Office Box 12642
Saint Petersburg, Florida 33733-2642, U.S.A.

Printed in the United States of America

A NOTE TO THE READER

This Study Guide is intended as a reference volume only, not as a medical guide or manual for self-treatment. To further enhance your skill as a Reflexologist, we suggest utilizing the books STORIES THE FEET CAN TELL / HAVE TOLD and BETTER HEALTH WITH FOOT REFLEXOLOGY, Reflexology Videos 1 and 2, and this Study Guide, in addition to your attendance at several International Institute of Reflexology Seminars.

The contents and opinions of this Study Guide are the result of extensive experience in Foot Reflexology and represent the theories of the International Institute of Reflexology. There may be some sections and opinions which are not in conformance to the theories and practice of the medical profession. The International Institute of Reflexology strongly suggests that self diagnosis not be attempted based on symptoms as they may be indicative of more than one condition within the body.

In any case of illness or even symptoms of a bodily dysfunction, it is advisable and essential that a competent medical practitioner be consulted.

It should also be noted that Reflexology is not a panacea. It is an adjunctive to medicine and must be regarded as such.

CONTENTS

Chapter One

THE SKELETAL, NERVOUS AND MUSCULAR SYSTEMS

THE SKELETAL SYSTEM

The skeleton is divided into the *axial skeleton* and the *appendicular skeleton*. The axial is made up of the skull, vertebral column, ribs, and sternum. Together these bones form the central core of the body.

The appendicular skeleton consists of the shoulder girdle with the upper limbs and the pelvic girdle with the lower limbs. The ones in this group that will be the most important for *Reflexology* are the bones of the feet and hands.

THE FEET: In the feet we have a total of 26 bones - 14 *phalanges* (in the toes), 5 *metatarsal*, and the *tarsal* or ankle bones which are made up of 3 *cuneiform*, and one of each of the following; *cuboid, navicular, talus,* and *calcaneus.*

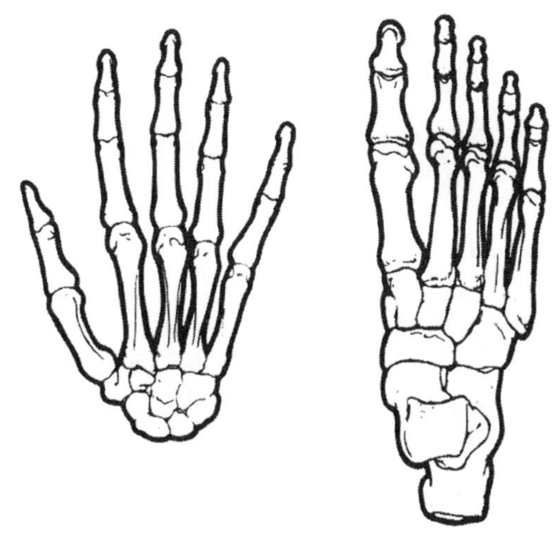

THE HANDS: In the hands we have a total of 27 bones - 14 *phalanges* (in the fingers), 5 *metacarpal*, and the *carpals* or wrist bones which are made up of one of each of the following; *trapezium, trapezoid, capitate, hamate, pisiform, triquetrum, lunate* and *scaphoid.*

Note in the drawing above the similarities of the bones of the feet and hands.

THE SKELETON: Now let's discuss the *axial skeleton*. Most of us just think of the bones as a support for the body and the protection for the organs, but they also contribute a great deal more to our well being. The skeletal system is one of the busiest tissues in the body. It is a *chemical factory* that is involved in the production of blood components, minerals, and other vital materials. Bones act as a reservoir for most of the body's mineral needs including 99% of the calcium and 88% of the phosphorus, plus copper and cobalt. The bones are factories that work around the clock making cellular elements of the blood.

THE SPINE: According to the book, BETTER HEALTH WITH FOOT REFLEXOLOGY, the spine "is part of the axial skeleton. It is a strong, flexible, rod-like structure which supports the head, give attachments to the ribs, and encloses and protects the vital spinal cord." The spine provides the supportive framework for the body which affords a wide range of movement. It has a siginificant impact on circulation, nerve supply, and general well being. It has been said a healthy, flexible spine insures a healthy body!

The spine is made up of 26 irregular shaped length and width bones called *vetebrae*. the first 7 are the *cervical vertebrae*. These have the widest range of movement. The cervicals support the head and allow it to twist down to look at the good green earth, or gaze upward into the heavens. Due to the mechanical marvels of the spine, we also experience 180 degrees of lateral movement.

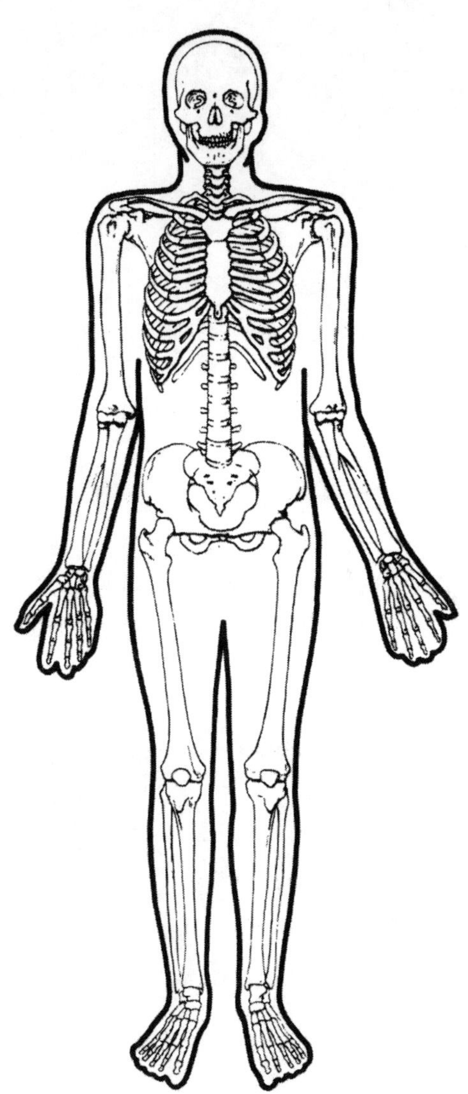

The next 12 vertebrae comprise the *thoracic* or *dorsal* section. It is within this section that the ribs attach to the spine. The degree of mobility found in this area is rather limited.

There are 5 vertebrae that make up the *lumbar* or lower back section. The bulk of the body's weight is carried here in the lumbar. We also find the greatest percentage of back ailments in the lumbar area.

The lumbar is followed by 1 *sacral*, which is comprised of 5 fused vertebrae, and 1 *coccyx* or tailbone. The coccyx is another trouble spot for the spine.

When we are born, the spine is straight. Two curves appear shortly after birth - one in the dorsal, and one in the sacral. Two additional curves will appear laer - one in the lumbar, one in the cervial. This will give the spine a slightly modified "S" shape. This "S" shape acts as a built-in shock absorption system. Every time we take a step, run, jump, or even reach down to pick something up, a tremendous amount of pressure is exerted upon the spine. So much pressure in fact, that without this built-in system, the spine would shatter at the simplest of movement. Interestingly enough, these *four curves* in the spine correspond closely to the four curves in the feet. If we place a view of the spine along one of the medical longitudinal arches of the foot, we can easily see how these curves match. This combined with the fact that there are 26 vertebrae in the spine, and 26 bones in the feet, confirms the view that *our feet can hold the anwsers to many of our back problems!*

There are 3 other structural components that we need to concern ourselves with:

DISC: The disc is a unique cushion found between each pair of vertebrae. Resembling a jelly doughnut, the disc protects the vertebrae from grinding one on another.

Each disc is actually a tough envelope of cartilage with a jelly-like interior. They are however, not indestructible. A severe jolt may actually smash one

of these discs necessitating its removal. A ruptured disc will allow its jelly-like contents to ooze out creating pressure on surrounding nerve endings and unbearable aggravation. When a tupture of this nature occurs, the muscle system will try and come to the rescue by forming a muscular splint around the rupture. This causes severe muscle spasms pulling the body in awkward positions. A ruptured disc may also irritate the sciatic nerve and cause great pain to radiate down the legs.

SPINAL CORD: Found within the spinal column, is the spinal cord. This cylindrical structure is the main path for nerve inpulse conduction. The spinal cord is vital to all types of sensation and movement. It is surrounded by 3 layers of sheathing, a fluid bath to help absorb shock, and the bony housing of the vertebra. Half of the nerves compiling the cord are sensory in nature - conveying information to the brain. The balance are *motor nerves* responsible for transmission of orders from the brain to the muscles. Also, there are some activities which occur strictly by *"reflex"* without the message having to travel the complete circuit to the brain. Anytime there is an injury to the spinal cord, there is risk of breaking this pathway of nerve transmission which may result in paralysis or extreme discomfort.

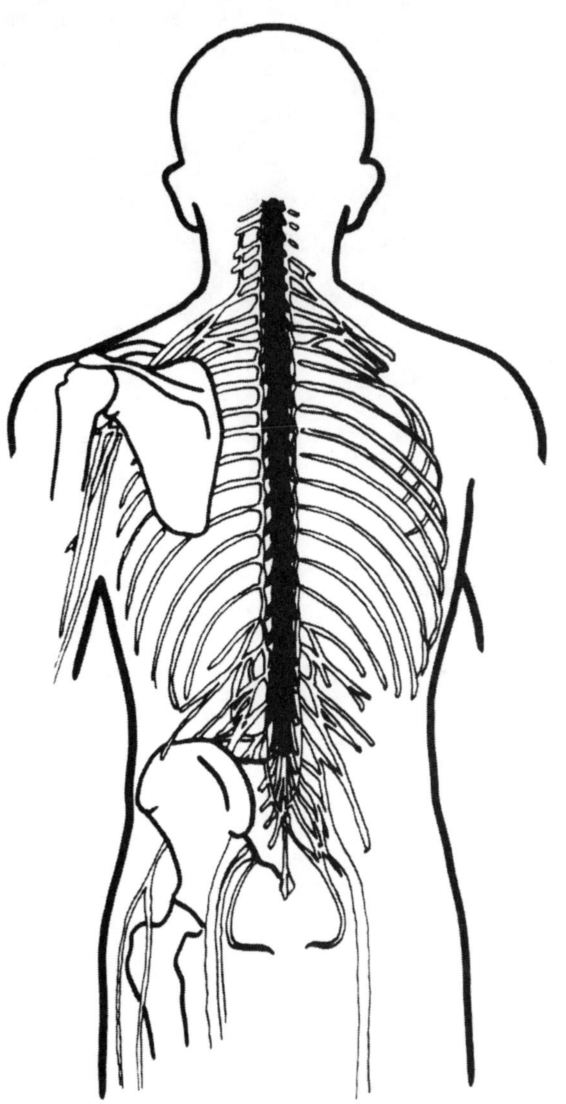

SPINAL NERVES: There are 31 pairs of spinal nerves each radiating off the spine. They are divided as follows: 8 *cervical*, 12 *thoracic*, 5 *lumbar*, 5 *sacral*, and 1 *coccygeal*.

THE CENTRAL NERVOUS SYTEM

The smooth operation of all body parts are under the joint control of the *central nervous system* and the *endocrine glands*. 50% to 60% of all problems are related to the spine. Hippocrates, the father of medicine, said *"Look to the spine for the cause of disease"*. Spinal problems are the cause for most of the lost man-hours found on the job today. The nervous system is the *balance for the entire body* and the link to all the systems. Just as the electrical wiring in a house makes everything run smoothly, the nervous system allows the body to run smoothly. The *spine* and the *brain* form the central processing unit of the nervous system.

NERVE DISTRIBUTION AND RELATED AILMENTS - These are also found in the book <u>BETTER HEALTH WITH FOOT REFLEXOLOGY</u> on pages 61 & 62. The nerve supply from the spinal vertebrae listed below show the areas and parts of the body they may affect. This text will show how these spinal nerve reflexes are used as *Helper Areas*, in addition to the *Direct Reflex areas*, for all of the organs, glands, and parts of the body.

THE CERVICAL NERVES:

1st and 2nd cervical nerves, coming from the 1st cervical vertebrae, go to the head, pituitary gland, scalp, brain, and ears. Conditions associated with pressure on this nerve are head colds, headaches, amnesia, chronic tiredness, dizziness, and muscle tension.

3rd cervical nerve, coming from the 2nd cervical vertebrae, goes to the eyes, sinuses, tongue, forehead, and mastoids. Conditions associated with pressure on this nerve are sinusitis, allergies, eye conditions, ear trouble, and fainting.

4th cervical nerve, coming from the 3rd cervical vertebrae, goes to the cheeks, teeth, and ears. Conditions associated with pressure on this nerve are neuritis, exema, and acne.

5th cervical nerve, coming from the 4th cervical vertebrae, goes to the nose, lips, mouth, and eustachian tubes. Conditions associated with pressure on this nerve are hay fever, catarrh, and blocked eustachian tubes.

6th cervical nerve. coming from the 5th cervical vertebrae, goes to the neck glands, pharynx, vocal cords and heart. Conditions associated with pressure on this nerve are hoarseness, sore throat, etc.

7th cervical nerve, coming from the 6th cervical vertebrae, goes to the neck muscles, shoulder muscles, tonsils, and heart. Conditions associated with pressure on this nerve are stiff neck, pain in the arm, croup, and tonsillitis.

8th cervical nerve, coming from the 7th cervical vertebrae, goes to the thyroid, shoulders, elbows, and heart. Conditions associated with pressure on this nerve are bursitis, thyroid problems, and colds.

THE THORACIC NERVES:

1st thoracic nerve goes to the esophagus, windpipe, heart, and the lower arms from the elbows, wrists, hands, and fingers. Conditions associated with pressure on this nerve are asthma, coughs, breathing difficulties, pain below the elbows, and the hand.

2nd thoracic nerve goes to the heart and coronary arteries. Conditions associated with pressure on this nerve are chest pain and functional heart conditions.

3rd thoracic nerve goes to the lungs, bronchial tubes (tespiration area), pleura, chest, heart, and breast. Conditions associated with pressure on this nerve are pleurisy, pneumonia, the grippe, and bronchitis.

4th thoracic nerve goes to the gall bladder, common bile duct, and the heart. Conditions associated with pressure on this nerve are jaundice, gall bladder problems and shingles.

5th thoracic nerve goes to the solar plexus, liver, and heart. Conditions associated with pressure on this nerve are fever, low blood pressure, anemia, arthritis, and adverse liver conditions.

6th thoracic nerve goes to the stomach. Conditions associated with pressure on this nerve are indigestion, heartburn, and nervous stomach.

7th thoracic nerve goes to the pancreas and duodenum. Conditions associated with pressure on this nerve are ulcers, diabetes, and often gastritis.

8th thoracic nerve goes to the spleen and diaphragm. Conditions associated with pressure on this nerve are leukemia and hiccoughs.

9th thoracic nerve goes to the adrenal glands. Conditions associated with pressure on this nerve are allergies, hives, and an inadequate reaction to stress.

10th thoracic nerve goes to the kidneys. Conditions associated with pressure on this nerve are kidney trouble, fatigue, and hardening of the arteries.

11th thoracic nerve goes to the kidneys ad ureters. Conditions associated wit pressure on this nerve are skin disorders and autointoxication (absorption of poison from the gastrointestinal canal).

12th thoracic nerve goes to the small intestines, fallopian tubes, and lymph circulation. Conditions associated with pressure on this nerve are gas pains, rheumatism, and lymphatic congestion.

THE LUMBAR, SACRAL, AND COCCYX NERVES:

1st lumbar nerve goes to the colon and groin area. Conditions associated with pressure on this nerve are inflammation of the colon, constipation, hernia, and diarrhea.

2nd lumbar nerve goes to the abdomen and its contents, appendix, blind pouch (cecum), and the thighs. Conditions associated with pressure on this nerve are cramps, appendicitis, varicose veins, and breathing difficulties.

3rd lumbar nerve goes to the reproductive glands, uniary bladder, and knee. Conditions associated with pressure on this nerve are bladder trouble, painful or irregular menstrual periods, change of life symptoms, knee pains, involuntary discharge of urine, and impotency.

4th lumbar nerve goes to the muscles of the lower back, sciatic nerve, and the prostate gland. Conditions associated with pressure on this nerve are lumbago, backaches, too frequent urination, and sciatica. The sciatic is the largest nerve in the body and affects nearly the whole leg, muscles of the back of the thigh, and the foot.

5th lumbar nerve goes to the lower legs, ankles, feet, toes, and arches. Conditions associated with pressure on this nerve are cold feet, weakness and poor circulation in the legs, weak or swollen ankles, and leg cramps.

The 5 sacral nerves goes to the hip bones and buttocks. Conditions associated with pressure on these nerves are curvature of the spine and sacroiliac strain.

The coccygeal nerve goes to the rectum and anus. Conditions associated with pressure of this nerve are hemorrhoids, pain at the end of the spine, and anal itch.

NOTE: Very few conditions listed here are wholly under the control of any one nerve. *Remember, when one end of the spine is affected it often affects the other end.* The spinal cord and its nerves serve the body every minute of every day. Pressure on these nerves can come from injuries, tight muscles, scar tissue, subluxations, and other causes. Emotions have a strong influence on the spine for they tighten muscles and cause spasms along the spinal column. The spine and its nerves are an engineering marvel.

THE BRAIN: The major nerves, of which there are 43, actually arise in the central nervous system; 12 pairs from the underside of the brain (*cranial nerves*) and 31 pairs from the spinal cord (*spinal nerves*). The cranial nerves are: 1. olfactory (smell), 2. optic (vision), 3. oculomotor (eye movements), 4. trochlear (eye movements), 5. trigeminal (mastication), 6. abducens (eye muscle movement), 7. facial (taste, facial expression), 8. vestibulocochlear (hearing, equilibrium), 9. glossopharyngeal (swallowing, taste, saliva secretion), 10. vagus (hunger, pain, respiratory reflexes, swallowing, actions of internal organs), 11. accessory (movement of head, shoulders, pharynx, larynx), and 12. hypoglossal (movements of the tongue). All excepting the first two cranial nerves originate in the brain stem. The trochlear nerve is the smallest, the trigeminal is the largest, and the vagus is the longest and most widely distributed.

The brain is composed of two symmetrical hemispheres. The *left hemisphere* controls the right side of the body and the *right hemisphere* controls the left side of the body. The brain constitutes about 1/50th of the body weight and lies within the cranial cavity. The *hypothalamus* lies at the base of the brain and is a collection of specialized nerve centers which connect to important areas of the

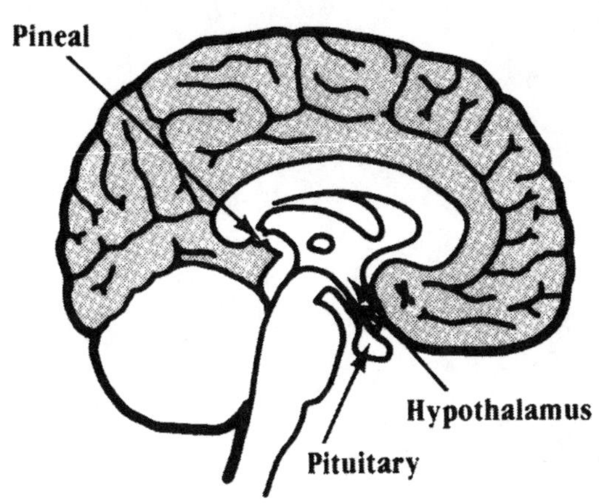

brain, as well as with the pituitary gland. It is also closely linked to the endocrine system. Immediately below is the *thalamus* that acts as an exchange between the spinal cord and the cerebral hemisphere of the brain.

The functions of the brain are the regulation of body activities, the center of consciousness, the seat of both our sensations and emotions, the source of voluntary acts, and the center for thought, reasoning, and memory.

THE MUSCULAR SYSTEM

The muscular system is the part of the body that contracts and relaxes giving the body movement and posture. There are 3 different kinds of muscles;

skeletal or voluntary (also called striated or striped), *smooth* or involuntary, and the *cardiac* muscle. The cardiac muscle is involuntary muscle, possessing the striated appearance of voluntary muscle.

Muscle functions are usually divided into 2 kinds; *voluntary* and *involuntary*. Voluntary muscles make up bout 25% of the body's weight. They are like springs attached at various points to the skeleton and control our movement. The *diaphragm*, as a voluntary muscle, is a large umbrella-shaped muscular band that is necessary for respiration. Involuntary muscles are not under the conscious control of the brain, but are responsible for such things as the muscular contractions required in the process of digestion.

Muscles can be attached directly to the bone or indirectly by *tendons*. A tendon is a dense, cylindrical or flat cord of connective-tissue that connects the facia of a muscle to a bone. Tendons are very strong and inelastic. At one end they are formed from the belly of the muscle and at the other they are firmly tethered to the bone.

We also have *ligaments* that are a form of connective tissue that hold bone to bone, and unlike tendons, can stretch very slightly. The bones at a joint are moved by muscles. These are joined to the bones by tendons, which cannot stretch. Ligaments, which can stretch very slightly, join the two bones that form the joint and keep them in place by restricting the movement they can make. Without ligaments bones would become dislocated very easily.

Ligaments are also found in the abdomen where they hold the organs such as the liver and uterus in place, where a degree of movement is necessary. There are also ligaments found the the breast that support the weight of the breast and prevent sagging.

We are usually unaware of the existence of ligaments until we injure one. A strained or sprained ligament makes its presence felt and is as painful as a broken bone.

When the muscles, tendons, and ligaments become over worked we experience a tired sensation or fatigue. Some causes for this fatigue are, over exertion, lack of proper nutrition (especially protiens, minerals and vitamins), poor circulation, inactivity, infections. etc.

Chapter One - Quiz

1. Name the 5 parts of the spine. ________________, ____________________

    ____________________________, _________________ and ______________.

2. The spine is made up of __________ (number) bones.

3. There are ______ pairs of spinal nerves and _______ pairs of cranial nerves.

4. There are ______ bones in the feet and ______ bones in the hands.

5. The body is divided into an _________ portion and an appendicular portion.

6. The 3 types of muscles are _________, _________ and _______________

7. The thoracic and abdominal cavities are separated by a broad muscle

    called the _____________________________.

8. _____________________ tissue specializes in moving the body and its parts.

9. _____________________ tissue receives and transmits messages to various

    parts of the body so they can cimmunicate with one another.

10. ___________________ are connective tissue that hold bone to bone.

11. ___________________ attach the muscles to bones.

12. There are __________ (number) phalanges in both the hands and feet.

13. There are __________ (number) metacarpal bones in each hand.

14. Between each of the vertebrae are ____________ which protect the
    vertebrae from grinding one on another.

THE CARDIOVASCULAR / CIRCULATORY SYSTEM

The primary task of the heart (that magnificent muscle) is pumping vital nutrients and oxygen to all the tissues of the body and in turn, carrying away their waste products, including carbon dioxide. It causes blood to circulate through a system of arteries, capillaries, and veins. Certainly a noble and life sustaining task at that. The heart is an organ that should be given great consideration.

If we were to open up the body to view the heart, we would find a hollow muscular organ about the size of your fist. It is red-brown in color and averages a weight of 4 ounces. It becomes immediately apparent that it is not "valentine" in shape as we are led to believe! Approximately one-third of the heart is situated on the right side of the midline of the body, with the remaining two-thirds to the left. This almost pear-shaped organ is suspended here by ligaments, and measures an average of 6 inches long, and at the widest point, 4 inches across.

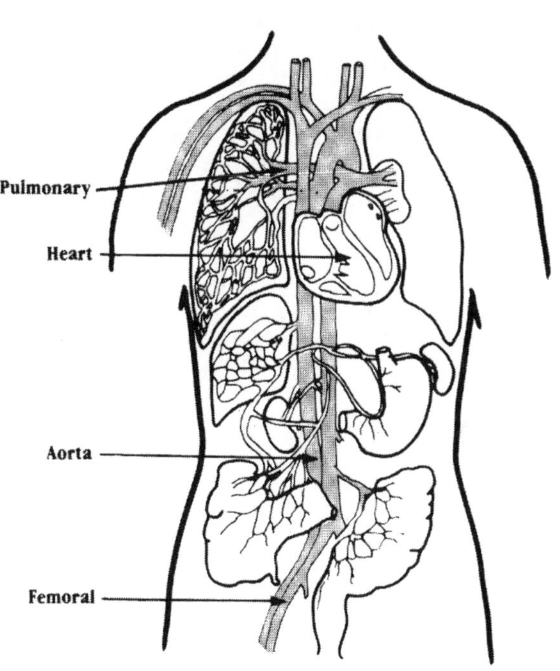

THE HEART: The heart has four main chambers for pumping the blood which are arranged in pairs. The right side of the heart, composed of the *right atrium* and *right ventricle*, receives blood from the vein which has been collected throughout the body. It then pumps that blood to the lungs to exchange the carbon dioxide wastes for fresh oxygen. The left side, composed of the *left atrium* and *left ventricle*, receives oxygen filled blood and pumps it back into circulation. The heart keeps up this continual pumping action day in and day out. There is however a brief resting in each

heart beat or the heart would soon wear itself out! The pumping cycle consists of a contraction (called *systole*) and a resting/filling stage (called *diastole*). In terms of time it takes three-tenths of a second for the larger left ventricle to contract - pushing the blood out into the body. This is followed by a one-half second of rest! During sleep, a large percentage of the body's capillaries are inactive. This means that the blood doesn't have to be pumped through them. The heart beat then slows down from a normal 72 to as low as 55.

The heart is nourished by the same blood which it is responsible for pumping throughout the body. In fact, it requires one-twentieth of the body's total blood supply. The heart is fed by two coronary arteries, each with little branching "tree-like" structures. The widest part of these "trees" surrounding the outside of the heart are not much larger than a drinking straw. It is here that a *build-up of cholesterol* may occur in the heart muscle leading to what is called a myocardial infarction, or more commonly known as the death of the heart muscle tissue, or simply a heart attack.

THE BLOOD: The blood that is carried to the lungs is done so through the pulmonary artery. In the lungs, and in the many tiny capillaries found there, the blood makes a valuable life-sustaining trade. It gives up the carbon dioxide it is carrying to receive the all-essential oxygen the body requires. The pulmonary veins then carry the blood back to the left atrium of the heart where it begins its fantastic journey throughout the whole body.

As the blood enters the aorta from the heart, it starts a pressure wave along the arteries. This wave is the *pulse*; it travels much faster than the blood and arrives at the wrist in about a tenth of a second. The *arterial pulse* can be felt at the wrist or in other arterial areas. The average pulse rate is 60 to 80 beats per minute. The pulse tells you the rate at which the heart is beating, the rhythm or regularity of the heart beat, the volume or strength of the beat, and the tension of the artery wall. Factors that affect the pulse are: position (standing or lying), age, sex, exercise or at rest, and emotional state.

Cardiac muscle action produces electrical charges, that reach the body surface and can be detected and analyzed by the use of an electrocardio-

graph, which records waves correlated with atrial and ventricular contractions. Disturbances in the heart action are often reflected by variations in the recorded waves.

AILMENTS :
As previously mentioned, fatty deposits that build up in the arteries surrounding the heart are the number one trouble spot. Even if a total shutdown does occur, a clot may form and shut down part of the artery. When this happens, this portion of the heart muscle that the artery feeds dies. This leaves scar tissue - perhaps no larger than a marble. Sometimes the scar tissue gets as large as a tennis ball. Genetic studies show that a propensity to heart problems may be inherited. There are many things which can be done however to minimize the risk:

WEIGHT - Being overweight can be such a burden to the heart. Aside from the extra work it takes just to haul around extra pounds causing the heart to work harder, a pound of excess fat contains over 200 miles of capillaries through which blood must be pumped. This directly aggravates the blood pressure level. Take a fairly normal blood pressure of 140/80; the 140 (systolic) measures the pressure the heart works against while contracting, and the 80 (diastolic) is the pressure while at rest between beats. The lower this number, the more rest the heart is receiving. In overweight individuals it is not too uncommon to see this number rise to 100 or 120 or higher. This means that the heart is getting less rest - and working harder!

SMOKING - The main danger in smoking is the nicotine present in the cigarettes. The oxygen the blood picks up in the lung-oxygen exchange of a smoker is not as pure as the body needs, so the utilization of the oxygen is obstructed. The nicotine acts as a stimulant on the heart pushing up the heart rate from a normal 72 to as much as 80 beats a minute. In an average 2 packs a day smoker, the nicotine will constrict the arteries in the hands and feet raising the pressure that the heart must work against.

STRESS - Stress and worry aggravate the heart and increase the rate at which it works. Constant fretting stimulates the adrenal glands to produce adrenaline, which in turn stimulates the heart to work quicker. This is why adrenaline is given so often to cardiac arrest patients. It is hard in today's competitive society to learn to relax. But if we relax, all of our body parts and organs relax.

GOOD HEALTH FOR THE HEART:

EXERCISE - Regular mild exercise is very important. A mile or two walk a day would help to strengthen the heart. Climb a couple of flights of stairs instead of using the elevator. Regular exercise causes new blood pathways to develop. This give the heart a "back-up" crew if one pathway is shut down for some reason.

DIET - Be aware of the foods you eat, especially those which are high in fat content. Fat seems to promote the build-up of plaque in the arteries. Forty-five percent of the calories consumed by the average American are sourced directly from fats and refined sugars. This gives us a 50-50 chance of dying from clogged arteries. After a meal in which a lot of fat is consumed, fat globules in the blood stream seem to glue red blood cells together into a sludgy mess.

In summary - slim down, exercise regularly, cut down on the fats in your diet, and quit smoking.

Chapter Two - Quiz

1. The four chambers of the heart are ________________________________,

________________________, ________________ and ________________

2. The pumping cycle of the heart is called ________________ and the

   resting stage is called ________________________

3. Blood is carried to the lungs through the ________________ artery.

4. In the lungs the blood makes a trade of ____________________________

   for ________________________

5. The ________________ pulse is found in the wrist.

6. The primary task of the heart is pumping nutrients and ______________

   to all the tissues and carrying away waste products and

   ____

7. The test called ______________________ records the waves

   correlated with atrial and ventricular contractions.

8. ______________________ causes plaque in the arteries.

9. ______________________ causes new blood pathways to develop.

10. Stress and worry aggravate the heart and ________________ the rate

   at which it works.

Chapter Three

THE LYMPHATIC SYSTEM

The lymph-vascular system is another of the body's systems of vessels that carry fluid around the body. The lymphatic system is an *auxiliary* to our *venous system*. The lymph system consists of *lymph vessels, lymph nodes*, and *lymph tissues*. The lymph vessels are concerned with conveying excess fluid, foreign particles and other materials from the body's tissues and cells. This system is involved in dealing with waste and potentially harmful particles. It works closely with the blood, especially the white blood cells known as *lymphocytes* which are essential to the body's defense against disease.

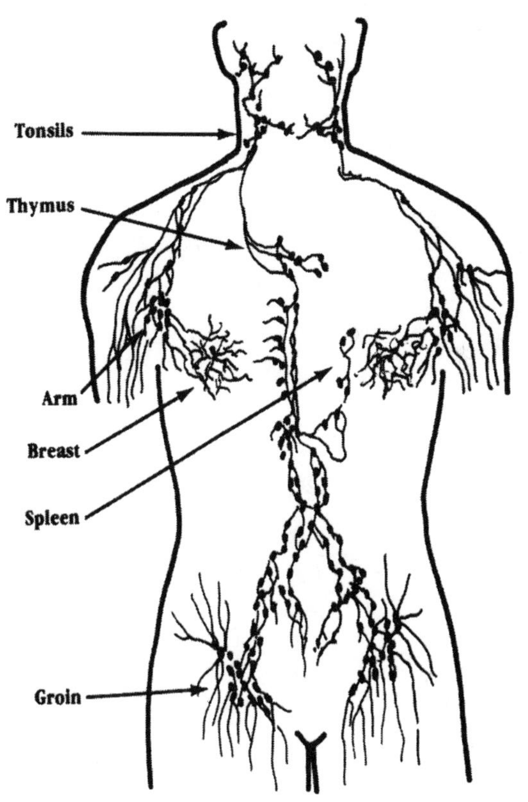

The function of the lymphatic system is to return to the bloodstream the fluid that filters out of the capillaries. This fluid, which resembles blood except it lacks red blood cells, is called *tissue fluid*. When it is collected into the lymph vessels, it is called *lymph*.

The lymphatic system consists of *lymph vessels, lymph nodes* and other *lymphatic tissue*, the *spleen*, and the *thymus* gland. Lymph capillaries originate as blind-end tubes in the interstitial spaces. They have the same structure as blood capillaries. These join to form the larger lymph vessels. The walls of the vessels are about the same thickness as those of small veins and have the same types of tissue.

The lymphatic system has *no pumping mechanism* like the heart. The flow

is facilitated by muscular activity that compresses the lymph vessels, forcing the lymph onward; by respiratory movements that compress the main lymph ducts; and by intestinal movements. *Moderate exercise* and *deep breathing* is needed to keep the lymph fluid moving. The lymph vessels have numerous cup-shaped valves that prevent the backward flow of lymph.

LYMPH VESSELS: These vessels carry electrolytes, proteins, water, etc. in the form of lymph. Lymph is a clear, yellowish fluid that bathes tissues and cells. The lymph vessels become larger as they join together, eventually forming two large ducts: the *thoracic duct* and the *right lymphatic duct*. The thoracic duct drains lymph from both legs, the pelvic and abdominal cavities, the left half of the thorax, head, neck, and the left arm into the left subclavian vein.

The right lymphatic duct is a dilated lymph vessel that lies in the root of the neck and opens into the right subclavian vein. It drains lymph from the right half of the thorax, head and neck and right arm.

LYMPH NODES: All the small and medium-sized lymph vessels open into lymph nodes which are situated in strategic positions throughout the body. The lymph drains through a number of nodes before returning to the blood. These nodes vary in size from the size of a pin head to the size of an almond. Lymph nodes occur in groups located in the head, face, neck, thoracic region, armpits, lower limbs, groin, pelvic, and abdominal regions. Inadequate drainage of lymph results in edema (swelling) in the tissue spaces. Infections and malignant cells may spread along lymph vessels.

The lymphatic organs, composed principally of lymphatic tissue, include the *lymph nodes, spleen, tonsils,* and *thymus.* Organic material is destroyed in the lymph nodes by macrophages and antibodies produced by B-lymphocytes in the nodes. Macrophages have the power to engulf foreign matter and filter the lymph, removing substances such as carbon particles, bacteria, tissue debris, and malignant cells. When this is incomplete they may stimulate inflammation in the node.

THE SPLEEN: The spleen is an integral part of the lymphatic system. Its main function is to act as a filter for the blood and make antibodies. The

spleen is a large gland-like but ductless organ that lies just below the diaphragm at the top of the left side of the abdominal cavity and is made up of lymphatic tissue. It is normally about 5 inches long, and lies along the line of the 10th rib. The spleen usually weighs about one-half pound in adults, but when enlarged it can weigh up to four and one-half pounds or more. It is supplied with blood via the splenic artery.

The spleen is one of the *main filters of the blood*. It removes old and worn-out blood cells as well as abnormal cells from the red blood cells. White blood cells and platelets are also filtered selectively by the spleen when it is necessary. It also removes abnormal particles floating in the bloodstream and therefore plays a major part in ridding the body of harmful bacteria. The spleen is also instrumental in making *antibodies* - proteins that circulate in the blood which bind on to and immobilize foreign protein so that white blood cells can destroy it. In people who have had bone marrow disease, the spleen and liver become the major sites for production of red blood cells. The spleen also *stores iron* which helps to build up the red blood cells. People who are deficient in iron are anemic. If the spleen has to be removed, the liver will take over some of its functions.

THE TONSILS: The tonsils lie in the walls of the pharynx and the root of the tongue. They are present at birth and grow rapidly the first few years of life, and then regress after puberty. They do not disappear completely. The tonsils play an important role in *maintaining the body's defense against disease*. This immunity is given by the lymphocytes processed by the tonsils. The tonsils also produce antibodies which deal with infections locally. Almost everyone will have suffered with tonsillitis some time during their life.

THE ADENOIDS: Adenoids are also lymph glands located at the back of the nose just where the air passages join those of the back of the mouth or pharynx. They are full of infection-fighting cells, the white cells. They are placed so that any infection breathed in through the nose is filtered by them and hopefully killed. The adenoids are present at birth, but they disappear before puberty.

THE THYMUS: The thymus is a *lymphatic* and *endocrine* organ. It lies in the upper part of the chest, just behind the sternum and extends upwards into the neck. It weighs about one-half ounce at birth and grows until puberty, at which time it starts to shrink. The thymus contains many of the

lymphocytes that are important in the body's defense against disease. Lymphocytes that enter the thymus mature and develop into activated *T-cells* that are responsible for cellular immunity. The exact ways in which the thymus controls its T-cells is not known. The only cells the thymus allows to develop are those that will attack outside foreign substances.

Much is yet to be learned about the nature and working of the immune response. It appears that when an invading organism enters the body it is taken either to a nearby lymph node or to the spleen by the lymph vessels.

Chapter Three - Quiz

1. The lymph-vascular system consists of _______________________,

_______________________ and _______________________

2. The lymphatic organs are _____________ and _______________

3. The lymphatic system is an auxiliary to our _____________ system.

4. What does the lymphatic system use for its pumping mechanism?

_______________________ and _______________________

5. The _______________ gland controls the T-cells.

6. The _______________ acts as a filter for the blood and also makes

antibodies.

7. The lymph vessels have what to prevent the back-flow of lymph?

____

8. _______________ are also aggregates of lymph nodules located in

the walls of the pharynx and root of the tongue.

9. _______________ are also lymph glands and are located at the back

of the nose.

10. Cancer of the lymphatics is called _______________________

11. Cancer cells are often transported from a primary tumor to other

regions of the body via _______________________

Chapter Four

THE SENSE ORGANS

The sense organs are used to make the body aware of its environment both inside and outside the body. Most bodily activities are adjustments to the environment by which we seek favorable conditions and attempt to avoid unfavorable or injurious conditions.

The sense organs are classified according to the information the body receives. There are sensations that give information about *internal environment* such as pain, fatigue, taste, hunger, thirst, nausea etc. The sensations that give information about the *external environment* are touch, pain, pressure, temperature, sight, hearing, and smell. The sense organs also give information about the body's position and movement - the sense of equilibrium.

The sense organs include: the skin for touch, the eyes for vision, the ears for hearing, the nose for smelling, and the tongue for tasting.

THE SKIN: The skin completely covers the body and helps hold it together. It protects the underlying structures from injury and bacterial invasion. It contains sensory nerve endings of pain, temperature, and touch, and is involved in the *regulation of the body's temperature.*

Another function of the skin is the *production of vitamin D*. There is a fatty substance in the skin which combines with ultraviolet light from the sun to produce vitamin D. This circulates in the blood and is used with calcium and phosphorus, in the formation and maintenance of bone. Excess vitamin D is stored in the liver.

The two main layers of skin are the *epidermis* and *dermis*. The layer below the surface of the skin is subcutaneous fat. The epidermis is the superficial layer of the skin and varies in thickness in different parts of the body. It is thickest on the palms of the hands and soles of the feet. There are no blood vessels or nerve endings in the epidermis. Hairs, secretion from sebaceous glands, and ducts of sweat glands pass through the epidermis to reach the surface.

The dermis is tough and elastic. It is composed of collagen and elastic fibers. The structures in the dermis are: blood vessels, lymph vessels, sensory nerve endings, sweat glands, hair roots, follicles and hairs, sebaceous glands, and involuntary muscles that are attached to hair follicles.

Blood vessels and lymph vessels form a network throughout the dermis. Nerve impulses that originate in the dermis are conveyed to the spinal cord by sensory nerves and then to the sensory area of the cerebrum where sensations are perceived. The sweat glands are distributed throughout the skin but are more numerous in the palms of the hands, soles of the feet, the armpit, and the groin. The most important function of sweat secreted by glands opening onto the skin surface is in the regulation of body temperature. The amount of sweat produced is governed by the hypothalamus. The hair is formed by the multiplication of cells of the bulb and as they are pushed upwards, the cells die and are converted to keratin. The hair above the skin is the shaft and the remainder is the root. The sebaceous glands pour their secretion, *sebum*, into the hair follicles and they are present in the skin wherever there is hair. There are little bundles of involuntary muscle fibers attached to the hair follicles. Contraction makes the hair stand erect and raises the skin causing "goose bumps".

The endocrine glands, especially the *thyroid* and *adrenal*, are keys to skin problems. The thyroid gland regulates the basal metabolism which is essential for normal growth and development. The adrenal glands regulate the water content of the body and influence inflammatory and allergic reactions throughout the body. Therefore, the adrenal glands help fight infection.

Nails are derived from the same cells as epidermis and hair and consist of hard dead cells. Nails protect the ends of the fingers and toes.

THE EYES: The eye is the organ of the sense of sight situated in the orbital cavity and it is supplied by the optic nerve (second cranial nerve). The space between the eye and the orbital cavity consists of bony walls and fatty tissue which help protect the eye from injury. The two eyes are structurally separate, but some of their activities are co-ordinated so that they function as a pair. It is possible to see with only one eye but the three-dimensional vision is impaired, especially in relation to the judgement of distance.

The chief structures of the eye are the three layers of tissue, and refracting media (cornea, aqueous fluid, lens, and vitreous body). The accessory structures of the eye include the eyebrows, eyelids, eyelashes, conjunctiva, lacrimal apparatus, and ocular muscles; and the orbits, or skull cavities, housing the eyes.

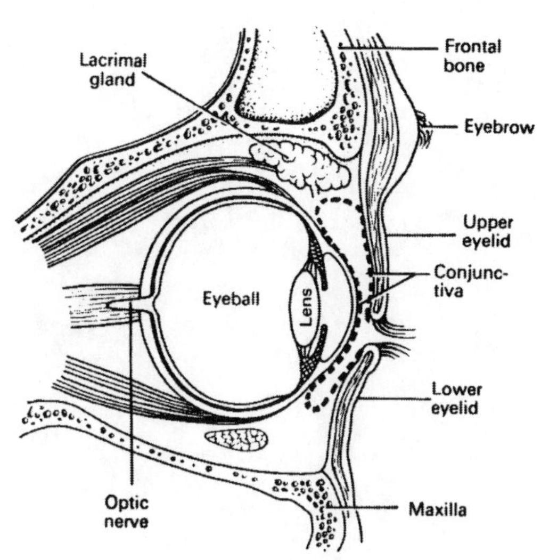

There are three layers of tissue in the walls of the eye: the outer fibrous layer - *sclera and cornea*; the middle vascular layer - *choroid, ciliary body*, and *iris*; the inner nervous tissue layer - retina.

The eye is perhaps one of the most complex organs in the body. When looking at a cut-away drawing of the eye, you can easily compare it to a camera. The cornea bends the light rays; the pupil, which is an adjustable iris, allows the proper amount of light to enter; the lens adjusts the focus on the retina. Light passes through the fluid that surrounds the lens and is focused on the retina. All the impulses received at the retina are carried to the brain through the optic nerve.

THE EAR : The ear is the sense organ of hearing and also gives us our balance. It is supplied by the eighth cranial nerve. The ear is divided into three distinct parts: the *external ear* (gathers sound), *the middle ear* (amplifies the sound), *internal ear* (converts sound vibrations into electrical impulses).

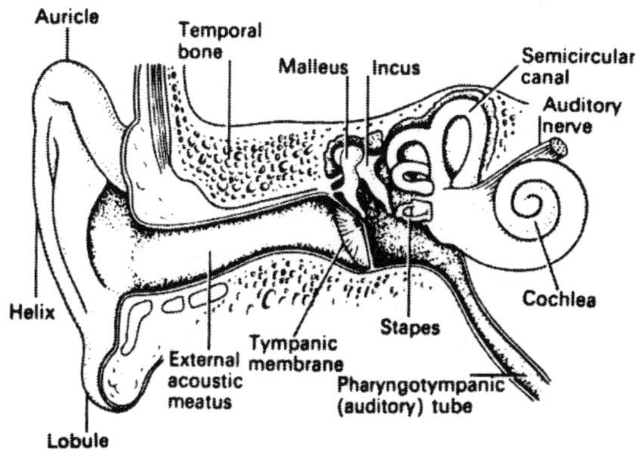

The external ear consists of the auricle, a structure of cartilage and muscle covered by skin, and the external acoustic meatus, a canal that leads to the tympanic membrane or eardrum. The sound that is gathered by the external or outer ear is sent down the canal to the eardrum in the middle ear. The eardrum is set in motion by the sound waves hitting it. The

vibration is magnified through a series of three bones called the *anvil, hammer* and *stirrup*. From there the sound goes to the internal or inner ear. The inner ear is made up of a complicated series of canals which contain sensory receptors. The main component of the inner ear is called the *cochlea* because it looks like a snail's shell. It is made up of a spiral canal which is filled with microscopic nerve cells. When a nerve cell vibrates, it sends an electrical current into the auditory nerve which then sends the impulse to the brain for translation.

Another very important function of the inner ear is that of *equilibrium* or balance. The three semicircular canals in the inner ear are filled with a fluid called endolymph. One of the canals reads up and down motion, one forward motion, and the third one lateral or side motion. When the body's motion causes the fluid in one of the canals to be displaced, the tiny hair cells read the message and send it to the brain, which in turn orders the body to get back into balance.

From the middle ear a narrow tube called the eustachian tube, opens behind the tonsils and equalizes the air pressure on each side of the eardrum. Popping in the ears when you rapidly descend in an elevator is caused by small movements of the eardrum through changes of pressure in the middle ear. The middle ear is often the site of infection, especially in children. The middle ear is directly connected with the mastoid air cells contained in the mastoid bone just behind the outer ears.

THE NOSE: The nose is the sense organ of smell, also known as the olfactory sense. It has two functions: smell and respiration. The sensory receptors for smell are found in the roof of the nasal cavity just beneath the frontal lobes of the brain. The olfactory area is made up of millions of small cells (olfactory receptors). Each cell has approximately a dozen fine hairs called cilia which project into a layer of mucus. The mucus keeps the cilia moist and acts as a trap for odorous substances. Olfactory nerve fibers send the signals of smell to the brain. It is in the brain that a smell becomes a conscious fact.

The nose also is used to clean the air before it enters the lungs. The nose also removes the irritants and particles from the air, warms it, and gives it proper moisture. The nose is capable of recognizing 4,000 different scents through the utilization of these special receptor cells in the roof of each nasal cavity.

THE TONGUE : The tongue is the sense organ of taste, or gustatory sense. Taste is the crudest of our five senses. It is limited in the information it gives us about the world around us. It's exclusive role is that of selector and appreciator of food and drink. It is helped by the sense of smell and vision. The loss of taste would be less of a problem than the loss of smell. Like smell, the taste mechanism is triggered by the chemical content of substances in food and drink. These particles are picked up in the mouth and converted into nerve impulses which are transmitted by nerves to the brain, where they are interpreted.

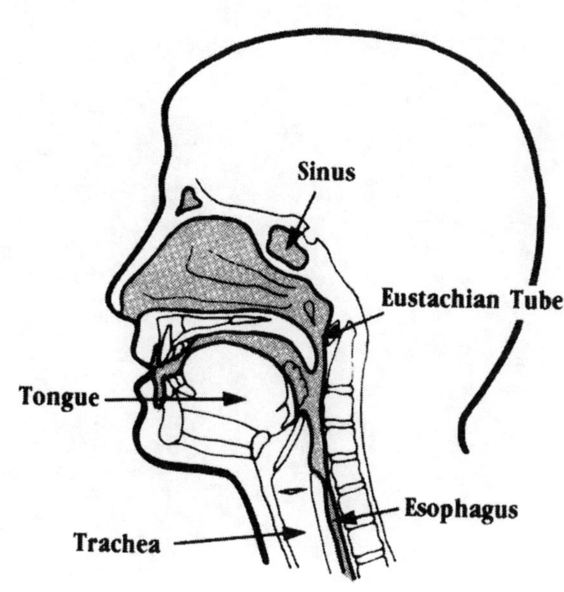

The taste buds are found inside the papillae, which are the projections found on the tongue. An adult has about 9,000 taste buds, mainly on the upper surface of the tongue, but there are also some on the palate and even the throat. The tongue recognizes four primary groups: sweet, sour, bitter, and salty. Sweet taste buds are located mainly on the tip of the tongue, sour at the sides, bitter at the back, and salty at sides and tip.

The tongue not only aids in the sensation of taste and swallowing food, but is also essential to speech.

Chapter Four - Quiz

1. Name 3 functions of the skin. ____

________________________________ and ________________________________

2. What part of the skin is composed of collagen and elastic fibers?

____

3. Name the 2 main layers of the skin __________ and ______________

4. Nails are derived from the same cells as the ___________________

5. The sebaceous glands secrete a substance called ______________

6. The _______________ nerve supplies the eye.

7. What part of the eye bends the light rays? _________________________

8. What part of the eye controls amount of light entering the eye?

____

9. Name the 3 parts of the ear _________, ________ and _____________

10. Name 2 functions of the ear ___________ and __________________

11. Name 3 things the nose does to the air ___________, ___________,

and __________________

12. The fine hairs in the nose are called ______________

13. The nose is the sense organ of __________________

14. What 3 things is the tongue essential for? ___________________

________________________ and ________________________

Chapter Five

THE RESPIRATORY SYSTEM

The term of respiration is defined as the union of oxygen with food in the cells, with the subsequent release of energy for work, heat, and for the release of carbon dioxide and water. The human body takes in oxygen and discharges carbon dioxide by the means of breathing, or external respiration. The exchange of oxygen and carbon dioxide between the blood and body cells and the utilization of oxygen by the cells constitutes *internal* or *cellular* respiration.

The organs of the respiratory system are: nose, pharynx, larynx, trachea, two bronchi (one in each lung), bronchiole (smaller air passages), two lungs and their pleura (coverings), and the muscles of respiration - the diaphragm and intercostal muscles.

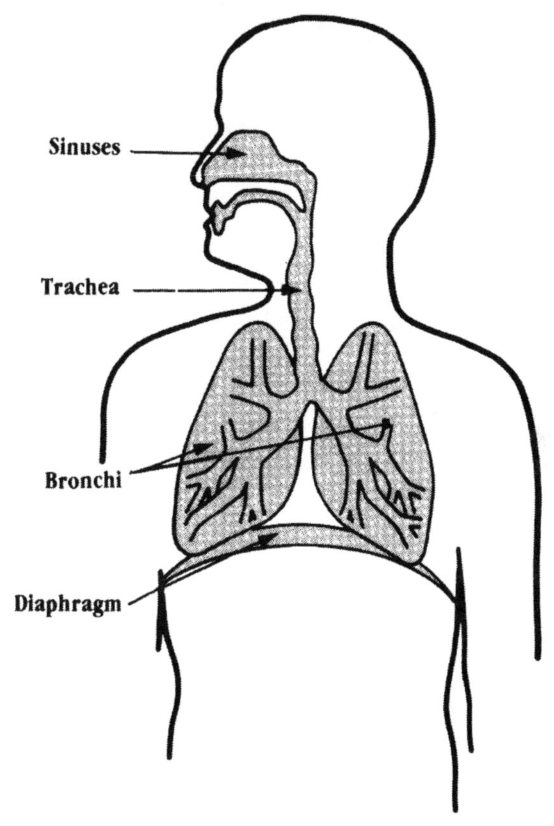

There are two types of breathing: *Costal* and *diaphragmatic*. Costal breathing is shallow and moves the chest upward and outward. It is seen in runners at the conclusion of a race. It involves the use of the external inter-costal and accessory muscles of res-piration. Diaphragmatic breathing involves the use of the diaphragm rather than the intercostal muscles. Diaphragmatic breathing is deep and is characterized by movement of the abdominal wall which is caused by the contraction and descent of the diaphragm. This type of respiration is usually seen during sleep. The diaphragm and other muscles of respiration are *voluntary* and can be controlled at will. However, normal breathing continues *involuntarily* even in an unconscious state. The automatic

breathing control is in the medulla oblongata - the bulge where the spinal cord taps into the brain.

THE NOSE: The nose is the first of the respiratory passages through which the incoming air passes. The function of the nose is to begin the process by which the air is warmed, moistened and filtered. The *paranasal sinuses* are air spaces adjacent to the nasal cavity that contain mucus glands and cilia that move the mucus into the nasal cavity. The air is warmed as it passes over the surface blood vessels in the interior of the nose; it is moistened by the contact with the mucus; and the impurities, such as dust and microbes, are trapped by the hairs that are moistened with mucus. This sticky mucus in the nose, throat and bronchial passages act like fly paper to trap the finer particles. But the real cleaning job falls to the cilia, microscopic hairs that wave back and forth. Their upward thrust sweeps the mucus towards the throat where it is swallowed or expectorated, thus filtering the air. The nose is an organ which is also part of the sensory system.

THE PHARYNX: The pharynx is an organ involved in both the respiratory and digestive systems. The air passes through the nasal and oral parts and the food through the oral and laryngeal parts. The air is further warmed and moistened as it passes through the pharynx. There are also nerve endings of the sense of taste in this area. In the pharynx the food and air passageways cross.

THE LARYNX: The larynx provides a passageway for air between the pharynx and the trachea. Here it continues to be further warmed, moistened, and filtered. One of the 7 cartilages found here is the *epiglottis*, which during swallowing forms a lid over the opening into the larynx to prevent the entrance of food into the larynx. This ensures that food passes into the esophagus and not into the respiratory passages. It is here in the larynx that you find the vocal cords or "voice box".

THE TRACHEA: The trachea or windpipe is a continuation of the larynx and extends to where it divides into the right and left *bronchi*, one to each lung. It lies in front of the esophagus. The arrangement of cartilage and elastic tissue prevent it from kinking or being obstructed as the head and neck move.

THE BRONCHI: The two bronchi are formed when the trachea divides. The right bronchus is wider and shorter than the left and it lies in a more vertical position. After entering the right lung it divides into three branches, one to each lobe. Then each branch subdivides into numerous smaller branches. The left bronchus is about twice as long and narrower than the right. After entering the left lung it divides into two branches, one to each lobe. Then each branch subdivides into progressively smaller branches.

THE LUNGS: There are two lungs, one on each side of the body in the thoracic cavity. The right lung is divided into three lobes: superior, middle, and *inferior*. The left lung has only two lobes: *superior* and *inferior*. The two primary bronchi enter each lung through the hilum, on the medial surface, along with the pulmonary blood vessels. Here the bronchi, arteries, veins, lymph vessels, nerves, and surrounding connective tissue form the root, from which the lung is suspended in the chest cavity. The lower surface rests on the diaphragm. Within each lung are millions of alveoli, alveolar ducts, bronchiole, and bronchi. The pleura, a double layered serous membrane, covers the lungs, lines the chest cavity, and covers the upper surface of the diaphragm. A serous fluid fills the space that separates the two layers so that the lungs can move without friction during respiration.

The function of the lung is to receive oxygen-poor blood from the heart. This blood passes through tiny capillaries in the lungs where it picks oxygen from the alveoli and makes a chemical trade-off: carbon dioxide from the cells for fresh oxygen.

EFFECTS OF SMOKING - If you could see the cilia in action, you would see what happens when someone inhales cigarette smoke into the lungs. The wave-like motion of those hairs stops and temporary paralysis occurs. If this continues long enough, the cilia wither and die - never to be replaced. After about 30 years of smoking most of the cilia would be destroyed and the mucus membrane would have thickened to many times their size. Without the upward motion of the cilia the mucus would drop down into the lungs instead of being carried upward to be expelled. This mucus would fill the air sacs and eventually suffocate the smoker. The smoker's cough is a defense mechanism as it helps to raise the mucus from the lungs.

After many years of breathing in smoke, air pollution, car fumes, pesticides, etc. the walls of the lungs and the air sacs loose their elasticity and don't collapse the way they used to when one exhales. The oxygen is inhaled but the carbon dioxide can't be exhaled. This is the cause of emphysema. The lungs can't be re-built, so it is too late to quit smoking when the signs of emphysema are present. Quitting should be established before these signs are there. Exercise is the best thing one can do for their lungs as exercise makes you breathe deeper and exhale more fully. Another good exercise for the lungs would be to take a big deep breath and exhale through the mouth, pushing with the diaphragm until all the air is expelled. Do this two or three times a day. This will take out all the bad air that has been taken in during the day.

Chapter Five - Quiz

1. The exchange of oxygen and carbon dioxide is called _______________

2. The 2 types of breathing are _______________ and _________________

3. The muscles used for respiration are __________ and _____________

4. The _____________________ are air spaces adjacent to the nasal cavity

    and they contain _______________ glands.

5. The _____________________ is an organ of the Respiratory and Digestive

    systems.

6. The epiglottis is found in the _________________________________

7. The trachea is also called the _________________________________

8. The "voice box" is found in the _________________________________

9. The lungs are found in the _______________________________ of the body.

10. The 3 lobes of the right lung are _______________ , _________________

    and _______________________

11. The blood passes through tiny _________________ in the lungs where

    it picks up _______________ from the _____________________

12. The tiny hairs found in the lungs are called _____________________

13. The _____________________ is a serous membrane that covers the lungs.

14. The trachea divides into 2 _________________ as it enters the lungs.

Chapter Six

THE DIGESTIVE SYSTEM

Digestion is the process which breaks down food into substances that can be absorbed and used by the body for energy, growth, and repair. The body either absorbs and uses these materials, stores them for later use, or eliminates them as waste products. The digestion depends on the enzymes that are produced by the organs attached to the digestive tract. These organs are also responsible for many of the chemical reactions involved in digestion.

The *alimentary tract* consists of: mouth, pharynx, esophagus, stomach, small intestine, large intestine (colon), rectum, and anal canal. The accessory organs are: salivary glands, pancreas, liver, and gall bladder.

All forms of life, whether plant, animal, or human, need certain types of food to keep them alive. With the exception of water, all of these food substances must be altered in some way before being absorbed into the bloodstream. This process takes place within the alimentary canal (digestive tract) where the food is first digested, then absorbed into the body.

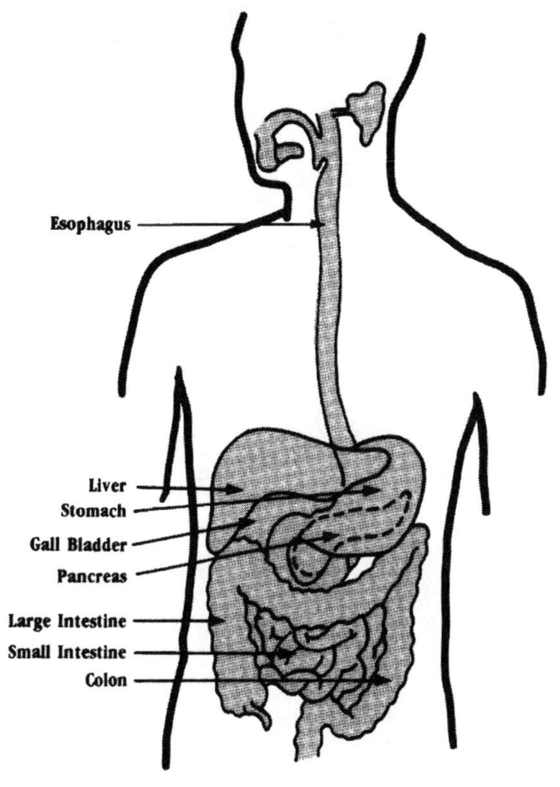

The mechanism of digestion is very intricate. It is largely dependent upon the nervous system. The sight and smell of food instantly cause our digestive juices to flow. When the eyes see a lemon, the salivary glands begin to salivate and flow into the mouth in anticipation.

THE MOUTH: The mouth is lined with mucous membrane that contain glands which produce the sticky, clear fluid known as mucus. It is this mucus that keeps the inside of the mouth moist and helps the action of the salivary glands. The main job of the tongue is to present the food to the teeth and to mold the softened food into a ball for swallowing. When this is completed, the tongue pushes this bolus into the pharynx at the back of the mouth.

Digestion begins the moment the food enters the mouth. Chewing is the first act when the food is broken down into smaller fragments, thus allowing the digestive juices to completely carry on their work. Chewing also encourages the flow of gastric juices, aids digestion, and helps relieve nervous tension.

THE SALIVARY GLANDS: Digestion depends on enzymes which are produced by the organs attached to the digestive tract and these enzymes are responsible for many of the chemical reactions involved in digestion. The salivary glands usually produce about 3 pints of saliva per day. The main function of saliva is to help in the process of digestion. Saliva also allows us to taste our food and drink. The sensation of taste is created by the taste buds that are mainly situated in the mucous membranes of the tongue. Saliva, a watery secretion consisting of mucus and fluid, contains an enzyme called *ptyalin* and a chemical called *lysozyme*. Ptyalin starts the break down of starchy food into simpler sugars and lysozyme acts as a disinfectant to help protect the mouth from infection.

THE STOMACH: Food then travels in wave like motions down the pharynx, to the esophagus, and then into the stomach. The stomach is a *"J-shaped"* organ situated mostly (about 85%) on the left side of the abdominal cavity. It varies in size with the amount of food it contains. The stomach acts as a temporary reservoir for food, allowing the digestive enzymes time to act. It is here in the stomach where the mixture of mucus, hydrochloric acid, and the enzyme pepsin is poured on to the food. The amount of stomach juices released is governed both here and in the intestine by nerve impulses, the presence of food, and the secretion of hormones.

The hormone *gastrin* stimulates the stomach cells to release hydrochloric acid and pepsin so that the food can be broken down into peptones. The

mucus secretion prevents the stomach lining from being damaged by the acid. Gastrin production ceases when the acidity reaches a certain point.

Another important substance, simply referred to as the *"intrinsic factor"*, binds to vitamin B-12 in the stomach and is needed for its absorption in the small intestine. Pernicious Anemia may occur when there is not enough of this "intrinsic factor" available in the stomach.

Muscular action mixes the food with gastric juice before moving it on to the small intestine. The rate at which the stomach empties depends upon the type of food eaten. A carbohydrate meal leaves the stomach in 2 to 3 hours, a protein meal remains longer, and a fatty meal remains in the stomach the longest. When the contents have reached a suitable degree of acidity and liquefaction, the pyloric antrum forces small jets of gastric contents through the pyloric sphincter into the duodenum. There is a limited amount of absorption that takes place in the stomach. Water, alcohol, and some drugs are absorbed through the walls of the stomach into the venous circulation.

THE SMALL INTESTINE: The small intestine is divided into 3 sections: *duodenum, jejunum,* and *ileum.* The small intestine is continuous with the stomach at the pyloric sphincter and leads into the large intestine (colon) at the ileocecal valve. There are approximately 22 feet of small intestine.

The food leaves the stomach as chyme, a thickish acidic liquid. The chyme passes through the pyloric valve by muscular contractions or peristalsis into the first part of the small intestine called the *duodenum*, where it is mixed with enzymes from the pancreas and gall bladder by way of the common duct. The small intestine is actually an elaborate food processing and waste eliminator plant. It is responsible for converting foods into an acceptable state for absorption into the body. The small intestine is lined with mucus to protect it from the acid in the chyme. The surface area also has circular folds, villi, and numerous lymph nodes throughout the entire length of the small intestine.

When the acid chyme passes into the small intestine, it is mixed with pancreatic juice, bile and intestinal juice to neutralize the gastric juices from the stomach. The intestinal juice consists of water, mucus, mineral salts,

and an enzyme. The duodenum also receives the digestive juices from the pancreas, which consists of water, mineral salts, and the enzymes: amylase, lipase and peptidase, including trypsinogen and chymotrypsinogen. Pancreatic juice is strongly alkaline (ph 8). When the acid stomach contents enter the duodenum, they are mixed with pancreatic juice and bile and the ph is raised to between 6 and 8.

Bile, secreted by the liver, is stored in the gall bladder until it is needed. When a meal has been eaten the hormone CCK is secreted, stimulating contraction of the gall bladder and relaxation of the sphincter Oddi, allowing the bile and pancreatic juice to pass into the duodenum together. The contents of the bile are: water, mineral salts, mucus, bile salts, bile pigment (bilirubin), and cholesterol. The bile salts emulsify fats in the small intestine. Bilirubin is the waste product of the breakdown of erythrocytes that is reabsorbed and excreted in the urine. The presence of bile in the small intestine is necessary for the absorption of vitamin K and digested fats. The bile colors and deodorizes the feces and has a laxative effect.

The functions of the small intestine are: Onward movements of its contents by peristaltic action, secretion of intestinal juices, completion of digestion, protection against infection, secretion of hormones, and absorption of nutrient materials. Digestion of all nutrients is completed here: carbohydrates to monosaccharides, protein to amino acids, fats to fatty acids and glycerol.

The small intestine plays a *major roll in the digestion and absorption of the nutrients from food*. It takes processed food and puts it into circulation throughout the body: proteins and carbohydrates via the bloodstream and fats via the lymphatic system. It takes 3 to 8 hours to process a meal in the small intestine or "gut".

THE PANCREAS: The pancreas is located deep within the abdomen, behind the stomach and in front of the spine. Some of its neighbors include the liver, kidneys and large intestine. It is about 6 inches long and resembles a large dog's tongue. It weighs about 3 ounces. The pancreas is both an *exocrine* and *endocrine gland* and it is an *accessory organ to the digestive system.*

The islets of Langerhans are the endocrine part of the pancreas, consisting of groups of specialized cells distributed throughout the gland. They secrete the hormones *glucagon* and *insulin* into the bloodstream. The release of these hormones is related to the level of glucose *(blood sugar)* in the body at any given time. The combined action of insulin and glucagon keeps the blood-sugar at the proper levels and assures that glucose is burned and supplied as needed. The islets have no ducts and therefore allow the hormones to pass directly into the blood. The secretion of insulin into the bloodstream works in conjunction with the level of glucose (blood-sugar) that the pancreas has produced. It is the insulin which keeps the blood-sugar at the proper levels and sees that it is burned as needed.

The exocrine part of the pancreas consists of a large number of lobules made up of small alveoli. Each lobule is drained by a tiny duct which unite to form the pancreatic duct. These extend the whole length of the pancreas and open into the duodenum. Just before entering the duodenum, the pancreatic duct joins the common bile duct to form the ampulla of the bile duct. The opening of the ampulla into the duodenum is controlled by the sphincter of Oddi.

As a digestive organ, the pancreas produces some of the digestive juices which contain enzymes which help break protein into amino acids, convert starch into sugar, and break fat globules into a more soluble state. The pancreas secretes certain enzymes that help to keep the walls of the veins and arteries flexible.

THE LIVER: The liver is a secreting, spongy type organ weighing about 3 pounds. It has the ability to double its normal size under certain conditions. It is located predominantly on the right side of the body in the upper abdominal cavity below the diaphragm and protected by the rib cage.

The liver performs over 500 functions, taking over many of the functions of the spleen should the occasion arise. It also has the ability to regenerate itself in many cases; but if the liver fails, the body dies. Some of the functions of the liver are:

Converts glucose into glycogen in the presence of insulin, and change glycogen to glucose in the presence of glucagon as it is needed to maintain the blood glucose level.

Converts stored fat to a form in which it can be used by the tissues to provide energy.

Produces heat as it has a high metabolic rate. It is the main heat producing organ in the body.

Detoxifies poisonous substances and converts harmful substances such as ammonia into an innocuous substance such as urea, which is excreted in the urine. Its Kupffer cells are phagocytic (cells capable of ingesting particulate matter), removing bacteria and other harmful substances from the bloodstream.

Secretes bile which is made up of water, mucus, bile salts, bile pigments (bilirubin - the waste product of red blood cell destruction), and cholesterol. Bile is a lubricant for digestion and an emulsifier of fats.

Stores vitamin B-12; fat soluble vitamins A, D, E, K; water soluble vitamins, e.g., riboflavine, niacin, pyridoxine, folic acid; and iron, copper.

Synthesizes vitamin A from carotene found in some plants.

Synthesizes non-essential amino acids, plasma proteins, and most blood clotting factors from the available amino acids.

Metabolizes ethanol found in alcoholic drinks. Detoxifies drugs and noxious substances, such as toxins produced by microbes.

Activates and inactivates hormones, including insulin, glucagon, cortisol, aldosterone, thyroid, and sex hormones.

The chemical genius of the liver is basic to the strong beat of the heart, wide-open channels of the blood vessels, the soundness of digestion, sharpness of the brain, and strength of the muscles. The liver's cells influence the smooth functioning of all our organs. The liver provides

immunity to disease, is a great detoxifier, and helps fight infection. There is evidence that emotional tension, in addition to its direct effect on the blood vessels, hastens the process of narrowing the coronary blood vessels by interfering with the metabolism of the fats and overloading the blood stream with fatty substances - cholesterol - which thickens arteries. Cholesterol is an essential element of the blood that is manufactured within the liver and also absorbed from certain foods. Disturbances within the liver can be indicated by such conditions as continuing fatigue, irritability, sleeplessness, and liver pains.

THE GALL BLADDER: The gall bladder is a muscular, pear shaped organ that is attached to the underside of the liver and linked to the duodenum by a duct system. The walls of the gall bladder contain smooth muscles and in its hollow interior is stored some of the bile formed by the liver between meals. The liver secretes about 500 cc of bile a day. One of the more important functions of the gall bladder is the emulsification of fats, thus assuring their digestion and absorption. Another function of importance is that it serves as a lubricant in the intestines. The entrance into the intestine of the gastric contents of the stomach (containing hydrochloric acid and fats) not only stimulates bile production by the liver but also causes the previously formed bile to be expelled from the gall bladder into the duodenum.

THE LARGE INTESTINE OR COLON: The ileum or terminal part of the small intestine ends at the ileocecal valve which controls the flow of material from the ileum to the large intestine and prevents regurgitation. The large intestine is much wider than the small intestine and is approximately 5 to 7 feet long. The first portion of the large intestine or colon is the cecum and it is found on the right side. The appendix is located on the blind end of the cecum. The ascending colon rises from the cecum on the right side; the bend is the hepatic flexure, following across the middle is the transverse colon, the following bend is the splenic flexure on the left side of the body, followed by the descending colon and then the sigmoid flexure, and sigmoid colon. The final section is the rectum and anal canal, or anus.

The contents which pass from the ileum of the small intestine through the ileocecal valve into the large intestine are fluid, even though some water

has been absorbed in the small intestine. In the large intestine absorption of water continues until the familiar semisolid consistency of *feces* is achieved. Mineral salts, vitamins, and some drugs are also absorbed into the blood capillaries from the large intestine. The function of the colon is to move solid material to the anus for elimination.

There are large numbers of microbes in the colon which synthesis vitamin K and folic acid. Gases in the bowel consist of some of the constituents of air, mainly nitrogen, swallowed with food and drink and also as a feature of some anxiety states. Hydrogen, carbon dioxide, and methane are produced by bacterial fermentation of unabsorbed nutrients, especially carbohydrate. Gasses pass out of the bowel as flatus. Large numbers of microbes are present in the feces.

The feces pass into the rectum by mass movement where nerve impulses are conveyed to consciousness. The external anal sphincter is under conscious control so the brain can inhibit the reflex to defecate until such time as it is convenient. About 60 to 70% of the weight of the feces is made up of water. The remainder consists of indigestible cellular material (fiber), dead and live microbes, epithelial cells from the walls of the tract, some fatty acids, and mucus secreted by the lining mucosa of the large intestine. Mucus helps lubricate the feces and an adequate amount of roughage in the diet ensures the contents of the colon are sufficiently bulky to stimulate defecation.

THE INVOLVEMENT OF ILEOCECAL VALVE MALFUNCTION IN CONNEC-TION WITH SINUS AND RESPIRATORY PROBLEMS AND POSSIBLE ALLERGIC REACTIONS The connection between the ileocecal valve, sinus and respiratory problems, and general body weakness has long been recognized by many of the holistic and complimentary healing sciences, particularly Reflexology. The actual physiological processes involved have not been fully understood or investigated. A group of medical

researchers interested in Reflexology have found an answer which goes to prove the miraculous way in which the body operates as one unit, each part relying on another. One small dysfunction in the body can cause a disorder distal to the original problem.

The ileocecal valve is in actual fact a sphincter muscle preventing the back flow of toxic substances from the large colon into the small intestine. It also permits the gradual passage of small amounts of intestinal contents into the cecum. It should open and close rhythmically, but often due to weakness it does not close tightly enough. This allows various toxic substances to seep back into the small intestine, causing an interaction of various chemicals which produce, among other substances, sterol. These are complex organic alcohols including ergosterol and cholesterol. The body reacts against these chemicals by producing tryptophan, an amino acid. If this reaction remains constant, the body then counter-reacts by over-producing histamine (another amino acid synthesized from histidine). This elevated level of histamine then causes the multitude of symptoms such as sinus and bronchial problems and all the other allergic reactions common to mankind.

How does the ileocecal valve get weak or hyper-active? It is possible that a diet consisting mainly of refined and processed foods and all the various preservatives and additives used upset the ileocecal valve. People who change over to a vegetarian diet too quickly can also upset the delicate working of this organ. Perhaps food allergies are caused by a weakness of the ileocecal valve, and why not? This weakness can also be caused by an injury to the ileocecal valve when the appendix has been removed. The small intestine will absorb all the various toxic substances that are produced when the ileocecal is not working properly. This will cause the entire organism to react against itself, producing the symptoms that we know as allergies.

Chapter Six - Quiz

1. Digestion breaks down food for the body to use for _______________

_______________________ and _________________________

2. The gall bladder stores __________________ until it is needed.

3. Digestion begins in the ________ where food is mixed with _________

4. ___________ starts the break down of starchy food.

5. Kupffer cells are phagocytic and are found in the ________________

6. The hormone ________ stimulates the stomach to release _________

and _______________________________

7. The 3 sections of the small intestine are ___________, ___________

and _____________________________

8. The _________________ controls the flow of material into the colon.

9. Cholesterol is manufactured in what organ? __________________

10. The major roll of digestion is done in the _________________

11. The 3 flexures in the large colon are _____________ , ___________

and ______________________

12. Emulsification of fats is a major function of the _______________

13. The _________________ is both and endocrine and exocrine gland.

14. The islets of Langerhans secrete hormones ________ and ________

Chapter Seven

THE URINARY SYSTEM

The body has several methods of eliminating waste products which must be removed so that the body does not poison itself. This is done through various systems: the sweat glands in the skin, the lungs, the large intestine, and the urinary system.

The urinary system consists of: two kidneys, two ureters (excretory tubes), one urinary bladder for storage and expulsion of urine, and one urethra (duct from the bladder to the outside of the body). This system eliminates the toxins and poisons from the body by filtering the blood as it passes through the kidneys.

THE KIDNEYS: There are two kidneys that lie on the posterior abdominal wall - one on each side of the vertebral column, behind the peritoneum and below the diaphragm. The right kidney is usually lower than the left, probably because of the considerable space occupied by the liver. They extend

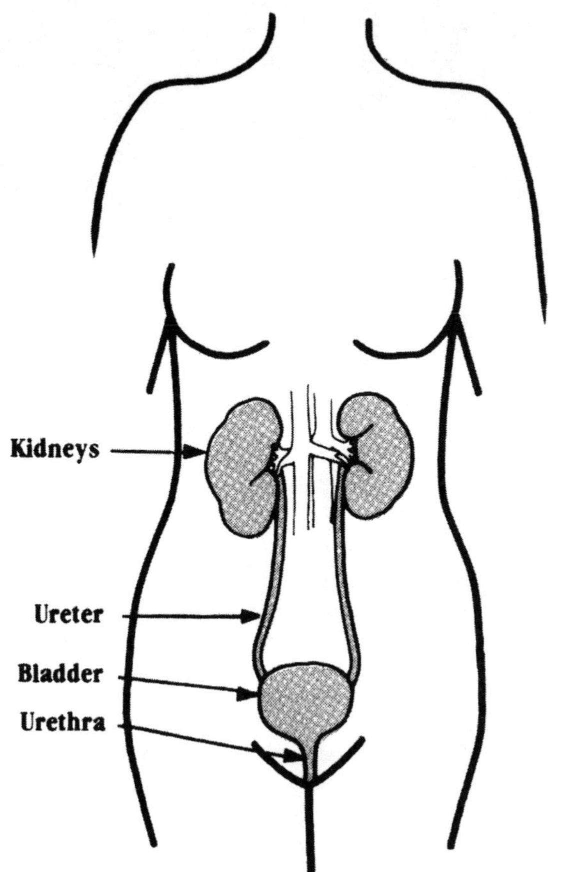

from the level of the 12th thoracic vertebra to the 3rd lumbar vertebra. The kidneys are reddish-brown in color and bean-shaped. These organs are embedded in, and held in position by a mass of fat. A sheath of fibroelastic renal fascia encloses the kidney and the renal fat.

The kidney substance is composed of about 1 million functional units called *nephrons*, each consisting of a renal corpuscle and a tubule. These uriniferous tubules are supported by a small amount of connective tissue containing blood vessels, nerves, and lymph vessels. The nephrons are the filters in the kidneys that filter all the blood in the body about two times per hour. About 98% of this fluid is returned to the body to meet its present demand for water. These filters rid the body of toxic substances and other waste products, including nitrogen.

Aside from the filtering of the blood, the kidneys must act as the *Master Chemists* in the body. They control the balance of sodium and potassium (electrolyte balance), the water balance, and the uric acid levels. Too little or too much of these has an effect on other parts of the body. Too little salt retained and the body would quickly become dehydrated. Too much, and the body begins to drown in its own fluids. Too little potassium and the muscular action may begin to falter. But, too much acts as a brake on the heart resulting in death. Urea and uric acid are end products of protein digestion. If too little urea is left in the blood stream, damage may result to the liver. Too much however, and uremic poisoning would result. As the urine accumulates in the blood, the body will fight to rid itself of this toxic substance. Gout is a form of arthritis in which uric acid appears in excessive quantities in the blood and is deposited in the joints and other tissues of the body.

The antidiuretic hormone (ADH) regulates the water permeability in the kidneys. ADH is produced by the hypothalamus and stored in the pituitary, from where it is released. ADH functions to regulate water balance in the body and, because of this, it helps to control the blood pressure. When the blood pressure is high the secretion of ADH is inhibited, thus less water is reabsorbed and more water is excreted. This helps to lower the blood pressure back to normal. If the blood pressure is low, ADH is stimulated and the tubules in the kidneys reabsorb more water and excrete less water. This helps to raise the blood pressure back to normal.

THE URETERS: The urine excreted by the kidneys passes through the ureters. They are about 25 to 30 cm long with a diameter of about 3 mm.

They pass downward through the abdominal cavity into the pelvic cavity, and through the posterior wall of the urinary bladder. The ureters propel the urine from the kidneys into the bladder by peristaltic contraction of the muscular wall. These peristaltic waves occur at about 10 second intervals, sending little spurts of urine into the bladder.

THE BLADDER: The urinary bladder is a reservoir for urine which lies in the pelvic cavity. Its size and position vary, depending on the amount of urine it contains. When it is fully distended it rises into the abdominal cavity. In the male, it lies anterior to the rectum; in the female, it lies anterior to the uterus and vagina. When the bladder becomes distended with urine, sensory receptors in the bladder are stimulated, and the desire to urinate is experienced. Release of voluntary control permits the discharge of impulses that bring about relaxation of the sphincter muscle and contraction of the bladder wall. As a result, urine is discharged through the urethra. This is urination.

THE URETHRA: The urethra is a canal extending from the neck of the bladder to the exterior. The male urethra is associated with the urinary and reproductive systems. In the male it is about 20 cm long and carries both urine and semen. The first portion is surrounded by the prostate gland and is about 2.5 cm long; this section receives the ejaculatory ducts. The second portion is about 1.3 cm in length and the shortest and narrowest, extending from the prostate to the bulb of the penis. The third portion is about 16 cm long and extends through the penis. In the female, the urethra serves only as an excretory duct. It is about 3.8 cm long and extends along the frontal surface of the vagina to its external opening (urethral orifice) located between the vaginal orifice and the clitoris.

Chapter Seven - Quiz

1. The kidneys are ___________ in color and are _____________ shaped.

2. The filters in the kidneys are called _____________________

3. Waste products are eliminated from the body through ____________,

_________________, ________________ and ____________________

4. Urine is stored in the ___________________

5. The _________________ are the "Master Chemists".

6. Antidiuretic hormone (ADH) is produced by the __________________,

stored in the _______________, and used in the ________________

7. Gout is a form of ______________________

8. The tube that connects the kidneys to the bladder is ______________

9. What organ is important for the control of blood pressure? _________

10. Relaxation of the _________________ muscle releases urine from the

bladder.

11. The kidneys control the balance of __________ and _______________

12. The end products from protein digestion is __________________ and

____

13. The prostate gland surrounds the __________ in the male.

14. In the female the bladder lies ________________ the uterus and vagina.

Chapter Eight

THE ENDOCRINE SYSTEM

The endocrine system *regulates homeostasis* of many metabolic processes; it consists of endocrine glands and tissues that release hormones. Endocrine glands are ductless glands that secrete hormones into the interspace of tissue fluid. The endocrine glands, together with the nervous system, are responsible for the control of most activities in the body tissues. They help the body to adapt to the environment. There is no direct pipeline from an endocrine gland to any one particular organ. Instead, the glands produce internal secretions which are discharged into the blood and lymph systems and circulated throughout the body to stimulate the target tissue and change some metabolic activity. These secretions are chemical messengers called *hormones* from the Greek, "I stimulate".

The endocrine glands are made up of:
1. Pituitary and hypothalamus
2. Pineal
3. Thyroid
4. Parathyroid - 4 parathyroid
    glands
5. Thymus (also a lymphatic
    organ)
6. Adrenal - left suprarenal and
    right suprarenal
7. Pancreas - the Islets of Langerhans (also a digestive organ)
8. Reproductive or Gonads - 2 ovaries and 2 testes

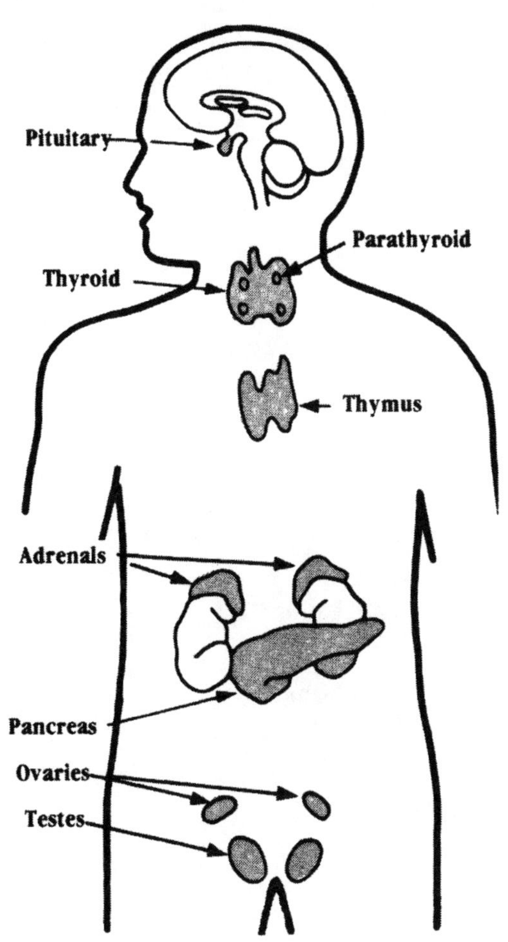

PITUITARY AND HYPOTHALAMUS: The pituitary gland and the hypothalamus act as a unit, regulating the activity of most of the other endocrine glands. The hypothalamus responds to feedback from both hormones and the nervous system and, in turn, controls the pituitary. The pituitary lies below the hypothalamus, to which it is attached by a *stalk*. The posterior lobe of the pituitary is a down-growth from the brain and the anterior lobe is an up-growth of tissue from the pharynx. There is a network of nerve fibers between the hypothalamus and the two lobes of the pituitary.

The pituitary gland is no bigger than the size of a pea. It is known as the "Master Gland" of the body as it is the only gland that secretes hormones that specifically affect all the other glands. In this manner it serves to monitor the activities of the other glands. Some of the hormones secreted by the anterior lobe stimulate or inhibit secretion by other endocrine glands while others have a direct effect on target tissue.

The posterior pituitary stores and secretes two hormones called *antidiuretic hormone* (ADH) and *oxytocin*. ADH is concerned with the control of water in the body. It acts on the tubules of the kidney, affecting their ability to retain or release water. When ADH is secreted into the blood, the kidneys tend to conserve water. When it is not secreted, more water is lost from the body in the urine. The oxytocin acts as a powerful stimulant to the pregnant uterus, especially toward the end of gestation. The hormone also causes milk to be expressed from the alveoli into the milk ducts. In males, it is thought that oxytocin may be concerned with generating an orgasm.

The anterior pituitary produces several protein or polypeptide hormones. Four of these are concerned with the control of other glands in the body: The thyroid, the adrenal glands and the gonads (testes in the male and ovaries in the female). The activity of the thyroid is triggered by TSH (thyroid stimulating hormone) while the cortex (outer part) of the adrenal gland is affected by the hormone ACTH (adrenocorticotrophic hormone). The levels of these hormones during times of stress is accelerated. The anterior pituitary also releases hormones known as *gonadotropin* that affect the sex glands. MSH (melanocyte-stimulating hormone) influences the formation or deposition of melanin in the body. Another hormone

produced by the anterior pituitary is GH (growth hormone) whose role is to promote normal growth. While this is most important during childhood and adolescence, the hormone continues to have importance in later life. It directly influences protein, carbohydrate, and lipid metabolism and controls the growth of foreign cells.

PINEAL GLAND OR BODY: The pineal gland is shaped like a pine cone that is attached by a stalk to the posterior wall of the third ventricle of the brain. It is believed to function as a light receptor. It appears to be the major site of melatonin biosynthesis. In humans its function has long been a mystery. New evidence shows that exposure to light results in suppression of melatonin secretion. The concentration of melatonin in the plasma is high in dark or very low light. Humans given large doses of melatonin become less alert and sleepy and therefore it may be important in promoting sleep. This hormone may also help control the onset of puberty in the male. Another hormone secreted by the pineal gland is *adrenoglomerulotropin* which is believed to play a role in the secretion of aldosterone from the adrenal cortex. Other substances found in the pineal gland are norepinephrine, serotonin, and histamine.

THE THYROID GLAND: The thyroid gland is the largest of the endocrine glands. It is shaped somewhat like a shield and is situated in front and sides of the neck. It produces hormones that are vital in maintaining normal growth and metabolism (the speed at which the body burns and uses cells). It also serves as a storehouse for iodine. The thyroid gland secretes two thyroid hormones and a hormone called calcitonin which works with the parathyroid glands. The two thyroid hormones are T3 (because it has three iodine atoms) and T4 (because it has four iodine atoms). Thyroxine (T4) is the principal hormone and is synthesized from the amino acid tyrosine and also from iodine.

The thyroid hormones:

Stimulate the rate of metabolism in almost all body tissues, except   brain tissue and lymph nodes. Stimulate the cellular production of heat.

Are essential to normal growth and development. Promote protein synthesis and enhance the effect of growth hormone.

Stimulate the mobilization of fat from adipose tissues and stimulate the oxidation of fatty acids by the cells. Also lowers the concentration of circulating cholesterol and triglycerides.

Increase the rate of carbohydrate absorption from the digestive tract and promote rapid uptake of glucose by the cells.

Stimulate the synthesis of coenzymes from vitamins.

May affect the response of tissues to epinephrine and norepinephrine.

Thyroid hormones are regulated by the hypothalamus-pituitary-thyroid control system. Internal environmental conditions, such as low thyroid hormone, or external factors, such as cold and stress, activate the hypothalamus, which secretes thyrotropin-releasing hormone TRH). This hormone acts on the pituitary and brings about release of the thyroid stimulating hormone (TSH). The TSH then stimulates the release of thyroid hormones such as T3 and T4. When enough thyroid hormone has been reached, there is a negative feed-back to the hypothalamus and TRH is no longer secreted.

Hyperthyroidism (an over-active thyroid) causes - loss of weight, nervousness, irritability, emotional instability, rapid heartbeat, very prominent eyes, and a toxic goiter.

Hypothyroidism (an under-active thyroid) causes - weight gain, dryness of skin, mental sluggishness, sleepiness, loss of energy, the cholesterol levels to rise, a non-toxic or endemic goiter (caused by a dietary iodine deficiency).

The thyroid has also been called the *third* ovary because of its important affect on those glands in the female.

THE PARATHYROID GLANDS: The parathyroid glands are embedded in the connective tissue that surrounds the posterior surfaces of the lateral lobes of the thyroid gland. There are usually four glands, but the number may vary from two to ten. They are about the size of the head of a pin.

The main hormone secreted by the parathyroid is *parathyroid hormone* (PTH) which regulates the calcium level of the blood and the tissue fluid. Appropriate concentrations of calcium are essential for normal nerve and muscle function, bone metabolism, plasma-membrane permeability, and blood clotting. The essential role of PTH is maintenance of a normal serum calcium level in association with vitamin D and calcitonin. It does this by exerting its effects on bone, kidney and gastrointestinal tract. In bone, it enhances bone resorption by increasing digestion of the bone matrix by osteoclasts. This effects the release of calcium from the bone into the bloodstream. In the kidney, PTH increases the excretion of phosphate and the reabsorption of filtered calcium. In the intestine, it increases intestinal absorption of calcium.

When calcium levels become excessive, calcitonin is released from the thyroid gland and quickly acts to inhibit removal of calcium from bone. Calcitonin operates mainly as a short-term but very rapid mechanism for regulating calcium level.

Hyperparathyroidism is often caused by small benign tumors called adenomas, which cause over-production of PTH. So much calcium may be removed from the bones that they are weakened and may be easily fractured. The kidneys attempt to excrete the excess calcium mobilized from the bones. So much calcium may be present in the urine that crystals of calcium precipitate and aggregate to form *kidney stones*. In severe cases the heart may be affected by the high calcium levels, and calcium deposits may form in various soft tissues of the body.

THE ADRENAL OR SUPRARENAL GLANDS: There are two adrenal glands, one situated on the upper pole of each kidney enclosed within the renal fascia. Each gland consists of a central portion, the adrenal medulla, and a larger outer section, the adrenal cortex which differ both anatomically and physiologically. The cortex is essential to life but the medulla is not. The medulla is more closely akin to the autonomic nervous system than to the rest of the endocrine glands.

The medulla releases the hormones *epinephrine* (adrenaline) and *norepinephrine* (noradrenaline) in response to stimulation of the sympathetic nervous system. They enter the bloodstream and are carried

throughout the body where they indirectly act as stimulants to various organs. Epinephrine and norepinephrine differ only in that epinephrine has a more prolonged effect because it is removed from the blood slowly.

The adrenal gland is referred to as the emergency gland of the body. The adrenal medulla prepares us to physiologically cope with threatening situations. These hormones increase the metabolic rate, elevate the cardiac output, constrict blood vessels to the skin and most internal organs, increase the strength of the skeletal muscles, and cause us to become more alert. It also enlarges the airways so that one breathes more effectively. Epinephrine and related drugs are used clinically to relieve nasal congestion and asthma. Acetylcholine released by preganglionic neurons triggers the release of these hormones. Anxiety or stress triggers the hypothalamus, which triggers the sympathetic nerves, acetylcholine is secreted, triggering the adrenal medulla, which secretes epinephrine and norepinephrine.

The adrenal cortex synthesizes and secretes more than 30 different steroids. The outer region produces mainly the mineralocorticoids; the middle region produces mainly the glucocorticoids; and the inner cells produce sex hormones, mainly male sex hormones, or androgens. All the hormones of the adrenal cortex are steroids synthesized from cholesterol.

Sex hormones are released by the adrenal cortex. Very small amounts of both *androgens* (hormones that have masculinizing effects) and *estrogens* (hormones that have feminizing effects) are secreted by the adrenal cortex in both sexes. In males, the amounts of these hormones released are so small that they have little physiological effect. However, in females, these male hormones may play some part in stimulating the adolescent growth spurt in females and in the development of female pubic and axillary hair.

Aldosterone is the principal mineralocorticoid. Its main functions are to maintain homeostasis of sodium and potassium ions and to regulate the water content of the body. It does this mainly by stimulating the kidneys to conserve sodium and to excrete potassium. They also exert important influences on inflammatory and allergic reactions throughout the body. Aldosterone also acts upon the sweat glands, salivary glands, and the digestive tract, stimulating retention of sodium and loss of potassium. The

net result of these activities is the maintenance of fluid and electrolyte balance in the blood and extracellular fluid which, in turn, affects cardiac output and blood pressure. When the level of aldosterone in the blood becomes too low, water leaves the body with the sodium, resulting in a dangerous reduction in blood pressure.

Cortisol (also known as hydrocortisone) is the principal glucocorticoid and is responsible for more than 95 percent of all glucocorticoid activity. The remainder of the hormonal activity is provided by corticosterone and cortisone. Glucocorticoids promote the metabolic breakdown of carbohydrates, proteins, and fats. Cortisol increases the rate of gluconeogenesis by the liver, decreases the utilization of glucose by the cells, reduces cellular protein and enhances utilization of amino acids by the liver, and promotes mobilization of fatty acids from adipose tissue into the plasma. The net effect of these actions is to make these non-carbohydrate nutritive elements readily available for energy.

The regulation of cortisol secretion involves a complex closed-loop negative feedback system. The hypothalamus reacts to stress by secreting CRF (corticotropin-releasing factor) which is carried to the anterior pituitary gland; in response, the pituitary secretes ACTH (adrenocorticotropic hormone) which stimulates the adrenal cortex to release cortisol.

Good health and survival depend upon the maintenance of homeostasis. Certain stimuli called stressors that disrupt the steady state of the body must therefore be dealt with quickly and effectively. Stressors can be from infection, disease, arguments, or even anxiety. Any of these can prepare the body for fight or flight. Some of these are short-lived and some continue over a long-term. Among the diseases linked to excessive amounts of adrenocortical hormones are ulcers, high blood pressure, atherosclerosis, and arthritis.

THE PANCREAS: The pancreas is usually thought of as a digestive organ. It is an elongated gland that lies in the abdomen posterior to the stomach and partially surrounded by a loop of the small intestine. It has both exocrine and endocrine components. The exocrine cells produce digestive enzymes and bicarbonates. *The islets of Langerhans* are the endocrine portion of the pancreas. There are more than a million small clusters of

these cells scattered throughout the pancreas.

Beta cells make up about 70 percent of the islet cells and produce the hormone, insulin. Alpha cells secrete the hormone, glucagon. Insulin and glucagon work together but in opposite ways to keep the blood-sugar level within normal limits, each balancing the effects of the other. Glucagon tends to raise the blood glucose level and insulin reduces it.

Insulin acts on cell membranes, stimulating the uptake of glucose, amino acids and fats. In addition it is associated with -

Conversion of glucose to glycogen in the liver and muscles.

Synthesis of DNA and RNA.

Storage of fat in the adipose tissue.

Prevention of gluconeogenesis and the breakdown of protein and fat.

Secretion of insulin is stimulated by increased blood glucose, amino acid levels, and gastrointestinal hormones, such as gastrin, secretin, and pancreozymin. Secretion is inhibited by sympathetic stimulation, adrenaline, and somatostatin.

The *delta cells* produce somatostatin, also called the growth-hormone-inhibiting hormones (GHIH), the same growth-inhibiting hormone released by the hypothalamus. Secretion of somatostatin is stimulated by several factors including increased glucagon and blood-glucose levels. Somatostatin inhibits insulin secretion.

Failure of the pancreas to secrete adequate insulin results in diabetes mellitus, a syndrome charcaterized by elevated blood sugar (hypergylcemia), weakness, loss of weight, profuse urination, and excessive thirst. Oversecretion of insulin causes low blood sugar level (hypoglycemia), a condition characterized by nervousness, sweating, extreme hunger, and fatigue.

Diabetes should be considered a group of diseases rather than a single

disorder. Although there is an inherited tendency to this disorder, it is thought that certain environmental factors trigger its actual development.

Two distinct clinical varieties of diabetes mellitus have been identified, *type I and type II.*

Insulin-dependent diabetes, referred to as type I diabetes, usually develops in children and young adults. It is marked by the dramatic decrease in the number of beta cells in the pancreas, resulting in insulin deficiency. Type I is believed to be an auto-immune condition in which the body develops antibodies to the beta cells. The antibodies destroy the tissue.

More than 90 percent of all cases are non-insulin dependent diabetes, or type II. This type develops gradually, usually in overweight persons over age 40. In many cases of type II diabetes, sufficient insulin is released by the islets of Langerhans. The problem is that the target cells are not able to take up the insulin and use it.

Hypoglycemia (low blood-sugar level) may be a warning sign of diabetes. It may be an overreaction by the islets to glucose challenge. Too much insulin is secreted in response to carbohydrate ingestion. About 3 hours after a meal the blood-sugar level falls below normal, making the individual feel very drowsy. If the reaction is severe enough, the person may become uncoordinated or even unconscious.

THE THYMUS GLAND: The thymus gland is both an endocrine gland and part of the lymphatic system. As an endocrine gland it secretes the hormone thymosin which promotes the maturation of the T-lymphocytes. More about the thymus is covered in the chapter on the Lymphatic System.

THE REPRODUCTIVE GLANDS OR GONADS: The endocrine portion of the reproductive glands are the gonads. The gonads are the ovaries in the female and the testes in the male. The ovaries produce estrogen and progesterone and the testes produce testosterone. They will be discussed in greater detail in the chapter on the Reproductive System.

Chapter Eight - Quiz

1. The endocrine glands produce a substance called ____________ which

   mean ______________________ in Greek.

2. The hormone responsible for elevating the level of calcium in the blood

   is ______________________

3. A type of gland that lacks ducts is an ______________________________

4. The ______________________ is considered the "Master Gland".

5. When the glucose level in the blood begins to fall, the ____________

   releases a hormone called ______________________________

6. The pituitary gland is regulated by the ______________________________

7. The hormone ____________ from the ______________________ gland

   affects the sex glands.

8. The ______________________ gland functions as a light receptor.

9. The ______________________ gland stimulates the rate of metabolism.

10. The ______________ glands maintain homeostasis of sodium and

    potassium.

11. The 2 types of diabetes are ______________________ , and

    ____

12. The endocrine portion of the pancreas is ______________________________

Chapter Nine

THE REPRODUCTIVE SYSTEM

The reproductive system of the male includes the two testes, a duct system, accessory glands, and the penis. The reproductive system of the female includes two ovaries, the two uterine tubes (Fallopian tubes), the uterus, the vagina, the vulva, and two breasts (mammary glands).

The reproductive systems function in the production of germ cells (spermatoza and ova) and in the bringing of the two germ cells (sperm and egg) together to produce a new individual. They also produce hormones that determine the development of male and female sexual characteristics. These hormones also play an important role in the development and behavior of an individual.

THE MALE REPRODUCTIVE SYSTEM

The testes are the reproductive glands of the male and are the equivalent of the ovaries in the female. The two testes are enclosed within a sac, the *scrotum*, located outside the abdominal cavity.

THE TESTES: The testes lie in the abdominal cavity close to the kidneys during embryonic development. As the fetus grows, the testes migrate downward through the abdiminal wall and take their position in the scrotum. In their descent they carry with them their ducts, blood vessels, and nerves (these form the spermatic cord). The passageway through which they pass is called the

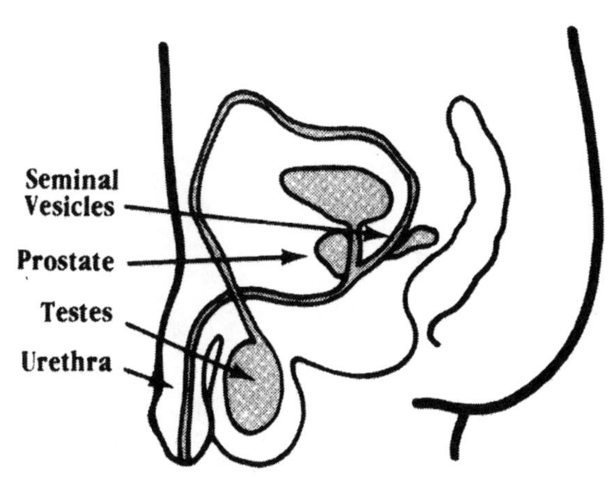

inguinal canal. It constitutes a weak spot through which contents of the abdominal cavity can protrude, causing a condition called an inguinal hernia. Sometimes the testes fail to descend and are retained within the

body cavity. When this occurs, spermatoza fail to develop because of the higher body temperature. When both testes are involved, sterility results. Descent of the testes into the scrotum should be complete by the 8th month of fetal life. Failure of one or both of the testes to descend into the scrotum is called cryptorchidism.

The function of the testes is twofold. First, they provide the site where sperm is manufactured. Each sperm contains all the genetic information for that particular male. Second, the testes contain cells which produce the male sex hormone, testoserone. This hormone gives the male characteristics such as the deep voice, male hair distribution, and the distribution of fat. These two functions are carried out by completely separate sets of cells; one function can fail without the other one necessarily doing so.

THE ACCESSORY GLANDS: The male accesory glands are the seminal vesicles, the prostate gland, and the bulbourethral (Cowper's) glands. The two seminal vesicles are located above the prostate gland and behind the bladder. Their secretory product contains prostaglandins, fructose, and a proteinaceous material for coagulation of the semen. It is a yellow, alkaline fluid of sticky consistency which helps to keep the spermatoza alive.

THE PROSTATE GLAND: The prostate gland lies in the pelvic cavity in front of the rectum and beow the bladder, surrounding the first part of the urethra. It consists of 30 to 40 alveolar glands with ducts leading into the urethra. Its secretion is a thin, opalescent fluid that is responsible for the odor of the semen. It contains citric acid, zinc, magnesium phosphatase, and a number of other enzymes.

THE BULBOURETHRAL GLANDS: The bulbourethral glands are two small, spherical glands that lie just below the prostate gland. Their ducts open into the urethra and secrete an alkaline fluid that provides lubrication.

THE URETHRA: The urethra in the male provides a common pathway for the flow of urine and semen. It originates at the urethral orifice of the bladder and passes through the prostate gland. The shortest and narrowest part extends from the prostate to the bulb of the penis and terminates at the external urethral orifice in the *glans penis*.

THE PENIS: The penis has a root and a body. The root lies in the perineum and the body surrounds the urethra. It is formed by three elongated masses of erectile tissue and involuntary muscle. The erectile tissue is supported by fibrous tissue and covered with skin. It has a rich supply of arterial blood. Under sexual stimulation this tissue becomes engorged with blood, thus bringing about erection. At its tip it is expanded into triangular structure known as the glans penis. In the center of the glans penis is a slit or opening, the external urethral orifice. The skin is folded over the glans penis as a foreskin or prepuce; circumcision removes the prepuce. Ejaculation from the penis ejects 200 to 400 million sperm cells, which retain their fertilizing ability for approximately 24 hours.

The male reproductive organs are stimulated by gonadotrophic hormones from the anterior lobe of the pituitary gland. The follicle-stimulating hormone stimulates the seminiferous tubules of the testes to produce spermatozoa.

THE FEMALE REPORDUCTIVE SYSTEM

The female reproductive organs include the ovaries, uterine tubes (Fallopian tubes), uterus, vagina, and external genitalia, or vulva. Also included are the mammary glands, which function in the nourshment of the young. The female organs are invloved in the production of ova, fertilization, development of the fetus, and childbirth. They are also a source of female hormones.

THE EXTERNAL GENITALS: The external female genitals are the clitoris and the labia, which togeth-er are known as the vulva. Most prominent among the parts of the vulva are the two pair of 'lips" or labia. The greater vestibular glands secrete mucus that keeps the vulva moist.

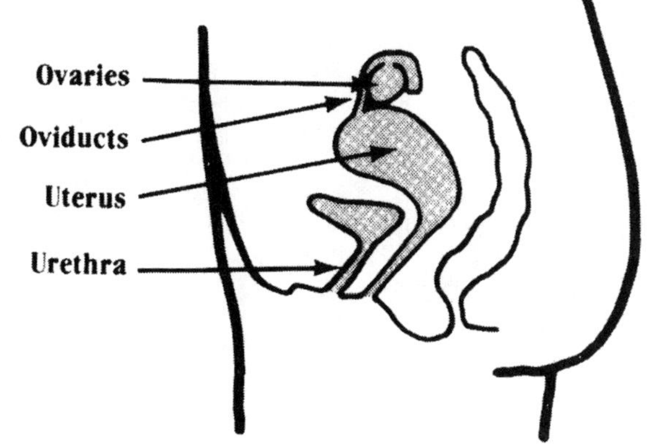

THE VAGINA: The vagina is a fibromuscular tube connecting the vulva to

the uterus. It runs obliquely upwards and backwards between the bladder in front and rectum and anus behind. It has not secretory glands but the surface is kept moist by cervical secretions. Between puberty and the menopause Lactobacillus acidophilus microbes are normally present and they secrete lactic acid. Lactic acid maintains the acidic pH, which inhibits the growth of most microbes that may enter the vagina.

THE UTERUS: The uterus is a pear-shaped, thick-walled, muscular organ suspended in the anterior part of the plevic cavity above the bladder and in front of the rectum. The lower end of the uterus projects into the vagina. This portion is called the cervix. The uterus seems to have almost no function before puberty and after menopause. During pregnancy, the uterus expands to allow the fetus to grow, and provides it with protection and nutrition. All the functions of the uterus are orchestrated by hormones released from both the pituitary gland and ovaries, and also by similar substances called prostaglandins which are released by the uterine tissue.

THE UTERINE TUBES: The uterine tubes or Fallpian tubes are two flexible, trumpet-shaped, muscular tubes, extending from the fundus of the uterus on either side toward the pelvic brim. The uterine tubes convey the ovum from the ovary to the uterus by peristalsis and ciliary movement. The mucus secreted by the lining membrane provides ideal conditions for movement of ova and spermatozoa. Fertilization of the ovum usually takes place in the uterine tube, then moves into the uterus.

THE OVARIES: The ovaries are the femal gonads, or glands. The ovaries are almond-shaped structures that lie on the lateral walls of the pelvis. Each ovary is held in place by strong, elastic ligaments. Just above each ovary is the feathery opening of the Fallopian tube which leads to the womb, or uterus. Although they are very close to each other, there is no direct connection between the ovary and the tube opening.

The ovaries are the parts of the female reproductive system which are designed to make and release mature ova, or eggs, From the first period to the menopause, normal ovaries release one egg each month. In their role as egg producers, the ovaries also act as hormonal or endocrine glands. The ovaries function under the control of the pituitary gland at the base of the brain.

The hypothalamus secretes luteinizing hormone-releasing hormone (LH-RH). This stimulates the anterior pituitary to secrete a hormone called follicle-stimulating hormone (FSH) which travels through the blood stream to the ovaries. FSH stimulates follicles and ovum development and also brings about the secretion of the hormone, estrogen.

After the follicle has ripened and burst, another pituitary hormone, luteinizing hormone (LH), is released to stimulate the development of corpus luteum and the secretion of progesterone. The job of corpus luteum is to help establish a pregnancy. If the egg is not fertilized within two weeks, the corpus luteum shrinks, progesterone production is turned off, and the lining of the uterus is shed as the monthly menstrual period (menstruation). If the egg has been fertilized, then the corpus luteum goes on working until the placenta is established and there is no bleeding.

About four or five years before menarche, the hypothalamus instructs the pituitary gland to secrete the growth hormone responsible for the sudden increase in a girl's height. She usually reaches her peak about two years before menarche and slows down just before her peirods begin. Pituitary hormones also prompt the ovaries to secrete estrogen which is largely responsible for enlarging the breasts, stimulating the growth of pubic hair, and for building up the uterine lining.

THE BREAST: The breasts or mammary glands are accessory glands of the female reproductive system. They also exist in the male but only in an undeveloped form. The breasts consist of glandular tissue, fibrous tissue, fatty tissue, lymph vessels, and lymph nodes. The glandular tissue is made up of about 20 lobes; each lobe is made up of lobules; the lobules consist of a cluster of alveoli; the alveoli open into small ducts that unite to form large excretory ducts called lactiferous ducts. The lactiferous ducts converge towards the center of the breasts where they form reservoirs for milk. There are narrow ducts that lead from these reservoirs to the surface at the nipple. The areola is the pigmented area in the center of the nipple containing numberous sebaceous glands which lubricate the nipple in pregnancy.

The breasts are quite small until puberty, when they grow and develop to their mature size under the influence of estrogen and progesterone. During pregnancy these hormones stimulate further growth. After the baby's birth, the hormone prolactin, from the anterior pituitary, stimulates the production of milk, and oxytocin from the posterior pituitary stimulates the release of milk in response to the sucking baby. The mammary glands are only active during pregnancy and after the birth of a baby.

Chapter Nine - Quiz

1. The mammary glands are located within the ___________________

2. In the male the tissue that surrounds the urethra is the ______________

3. Failure of the testes to descend through the inguinal canal is called

   ____

4. The hormone _______________________ is responsible for the male

   characteristics.

5. The hormones secreted by the ovaries are _______________________

   and _______________________

6. The site of fertilization in the female is _______________________

7. The lower, narrow portion of the uterus is called the ______________

8. What is the monthly period in the female called? ________________

9. The female gonads are ________________ and the male gonads are

   ____

10. The Reproductive system's function in the production of germ cells

   is called ___________________ and _______________________

11. The sac in which the testes lie is called the ___________________

12. The accessory glands in the male that secrete an alkaline fluid for

   lubrication are called ___________________________________

REFLEXOLOGY HELPER AREAS

The following pages represent a compilation of disorders with their associative helper reflex areas that will help bring the body to homeostasis or balance. They are listed **only** as a guide to help you become more proficient at Reflexology.

Reflexology is not intended to replace medical care. Consult your physician if you have a health problem. Reflexology relaxes tension, which in turn helps to improve nerve and blood supply and brings the body to homeostasis.

In no way is this to be construed as, nor used for, diagnostic purposes. Diagnosis is the prerogative of the physician. **Reflexologists do not diagnose, prescribe, nor treat for a specific condition at any time or in any manner.**

Helper areas are additional reflex areas worked to aid the specific region of congestion. They are the reinforcement you send to aid a specific reflex area. **Referral areas** are the reinforcement for Reflexology that allows us to work one part of the body to help an alternate part.

DISORDER   REFLEX AREAS

Acne
    Helper areas: All glands esp:
              Adrenals - for secretion of steroids (cortisone)
              Thyroid - essential for normal skin development
           Liver - to detoxify, remove bacteria
           Kidneys - to filter impurities from blood
           Intestines - to clean up toxins
           Diaphragm - for stress reduction and emotions

Adenoids
    Direct reflex: Lymphatics - adenoids are part of system
              Great toes - represent everything in the head
    Helper areas: Small toes - for fine tuning the head
              Pituitary - to control growth of cell
              Adrenals - to fight infection

Alcoholism
    Helper areas: Liver - to detoxify, metabolize the alcohol
                                Pancreas - for digestion of the sugars in alcohol
                                Diaphragm - to reduce stress and tension

Amyotrophic Lateral Sclerosis - "Lou Gehrig's" disease - ALS
    Helper areas: Brain - for central nervous system
                                Whole spine - for central nervous system
                                Great toes, small toes - for upper respiratory system
                                Chest/lung - for the lungs and breathing

Anemia
    Helper areas: Spleen - to control red blood cells
                                Liver - to filter the blood

Angina Pectoris (Coronary Occlusion)
    Direct reflex: Chest/lung - for heart, the area of pain
    Helper areas: Cervicals, thoracics - for nerve supply
                                Adrenals - relax heart muscle
                                Diaphragm - to relax and help breathing
                                Sigmoid colon - gas builds up in colon, pushes up
                                                on diaphragm, in turn, pushes on heart
                                              muscle

Ankles (swollen)
    Helper areas: Adrenals - to control water balance
                                Kidneys - for fluid removal
                                Lymphatics - to move fluid out of lymph tissue
    Referral area: Wrist

Appendicitis
    Direct reflex: Ileocecal - same reflex area as appendix
    Helper areas: Diaphragm - to relax the pain
                                  Adrenals - to help fight infection
                                Thoracics - for nerve supply

Arms (hands)
      Helper areas: Cervicals (5-6-7) - for nerve supply
                             Thoracics (1) - for nerve supply
                             Neck - for muscles in the neck
                             Shoulder - for nerves and muscles to extremities
                             Hip - one of four corners of torso, same zone
      Referral areas: Legs, feet

Arteriosclerosis
      Helper areas: All glands - to balance body chemistry
                             Pancreas - to secret enzyme that helps keep the
                                    walls of the arteries and veins flexible
                             Liver, thyroid - to control cholesterol
                             Entire foot - for circulation to the whole body

Arthritis
      Helper areas: Reflex to affected region
                             Kidneys - for uric acid
                             All glands - to balance body chemistry
                             Diaphragm - to relax, for pain

Asthma
      Direct reflex: Chest/lung - area affected
      Helper areas: Adrenals - for secretion of adrenaline
                             Ileocecal - for control of mucus
                             Diaphragm - to relax and help breathing

Bed Wetting
      Direct Reflex: Bladder
      Helper areas: Kidneys, ureters - urinary system
                             Adrenals - for muscle tone and control of kidneys
                             Diaphragm - for stress and emotions
                             Sacral/coccyx - for nerve supply

Bell's Palsy
    Helper areas: All toes - for the brain
                          Cervicals - for nerve supply to arms and hands
                          Neck - for blood supply
                          Diaphragm - to relax nervous tension
                          Parathyroids - normalize nerve function

Bladder Problems (Dysuria)
    Direct reflex: Bladder
    Helper areas: Kidneys, ureters - urinary system
                          Adrenals - for muscle tone and to fight infection
                          Lumbar (L-3) - for nerve supply
                          Coccyx - a tipped coccyx puts pressure on the
                                    bladder

Breast (lumps)
    Direct reflex: Chest/lung - reflex area for breasts
    Helper areas: Lymphatics - breasts contain lymphatic tissue
                          Pituitary - to control growth of foreign cells

Bronchitis
    Direct reflex: Chest/lung - area affected
    Helper areas: Diaphragm - to improve breathing
                          Adrenals - for the inflammation
                          Ileocecal - for mucus control
                          Lymphatics - as a cleansing system

Bunion
    Direct reflex: Work around, and then directly on the bunion
                          Work flexing the metatarsals

Bursitis
    Direct reflex: Reflex to affected area
    Helper area: Adrenals - for the inflammation
                          Parathyroids-for calcium buildup
    Referral area: Referral area to affected area
                                example - pain in shoulder, work hip reflex

Calluses, Corns
  Direct reflex: Work around and directly on corns and calluses

Carpal Tunnel Syndrome
  Helper areas: Cervicals (5-6-7) - for nerve supply
        Neck, shoulder - to relax muscles in the area
        Thoracic (1) - for nerve supply
  Referral area: Ankle

Cataracts
  Direct reflex: Eye reflex
  Helper areas: All toes - for fine tuning the eyes
        Neck - for blood supply
        Cervicals - for nerve supply
        Kidneys - they have an affect on the eyes
        Pituitary - to control growth of foreign cells

Chest Pains
  Direct reflex: Chest/lung
  Helper areas: Adrenals - adrenaline relaxes smooth muscle
        Cervicals, thoracics - for nerve supply
        Diaphragm - to relax tension
        Sigmoid - gas builds up, pushes on diaphragm, in
          turn, pushes on the heart

Childhood Diseases
  Helper areas: All glands - for hormone balance
        Diaphragm - to relax and calm the child
        Whole spine - for nerve supply
        Spleen, thymus - for immunity

Cholesterol
  Helper areas: Liver - manufactures cholesterol
        Thyroid - its hormones regulate liver's production
          of cholesterol

Chronic Fatigue Syndrome
      Helper areas: Pituitary - controls all the glands
                                 All glands - to balance the glands
                                 Whole spine - for central nervous system
                                 Lymphatics (esp. spleen) - as a cleansing system
                                 All toes - for the brain

Cirrhosis of the Liver
      Direct reflex: Liver
      Helper areas: All glands, esp. pancreas - insulin helps conversion
                                      of glucose into glycogen in the liver

Coccyx (backache)
      Direct reflex: Sacral/coccyx - for nerve supply
      Helper areas: Pelvic area - for relaxing lower back
                                 Hip, shoulder - four corners of torso help spine
                                 Cervicals - one end of spine affects the other
                                 Kidneys - often the cause of backache

Colds
      Direct Reflex: Toes - for sinuses
      Helper areas: Chest/lung - to improve breathing
                                 Adrenals - to fight infection
                                 Pituitary - for fever reduction
                                 Ileocecal - to reduce the mucus
                                 Lymphatic - as a cleanser

Colitis
      Direct reflex: Colon - area of inflammation
      Helper areas: Liver/gallbladder - for lubrication
                                 Adrenals - to fight infection
                                 Lumbar/sacral - for the nerve supply
                                 Diaphragm/solar plexus - to relax stress/tension

Conjunctivitis
    Direct reflex: Eye reflex - area of the inflammation
    Helper areas: All toes (esp. 2-3) - for fine tuning the eyes
                         Cervicals - for nerve supply
                         Neck - for blood supply
                         Adrenals - to fight infection

Constipation
    Direct reflex: Colon, especially sigmoid
    Helper areas: Ileocecal - for the mucus for lubrication
                         Liver/gallbladder - for lubrication
                         Adrenals - for muscle tone
                         Lumbar/sacral - for nerve supply
                         Diaphragm - for the emotions

Cramps (legs, feet)
    Helper areas: Parathyroid - for calcium absorption
                         Adrenals - for muscle tone
                         Lumbar/sacral - for nerve supply
                         Pelvic area - for nerve and blood supply
                         Hip/knee, hip/sciatic - for nerve and blood supply

Cramps (menstrual)
    Direct reflexes: Uterus, ovaries, fallopian (uterine) tubes
    Helper areas: Pituitary - regulates all the glands
                         Thyroid - is considered the third ovary
                         Adrenals - for the estrogen-progesterone balance
                         Lumbar/sacral - for nerve supply
                         Diaphragm - to relax stress and tension

Crohn's Disease

    Direct reflexes: Small intestine (esp. Ileocecal)

    Helper areas: Adrenals - for inflammation
    Ileocecal - helps colon empty
    Liver, gallbladder - for lubrication
    Spleen - to help immune system
    Thoracics - nerve supply
    Diaphragm - to relieve stress and pain

Croup

    Direct reflexes: Chest/lung and bronchial tubes

    Helper areas: Diaphragm - for relaxing and calming
    Ileocecal - for mucus control
    All toes - for sinus drainage

Cystitis

    Direct reflex: Bladder - area of inflammation

    Helper areas: Kidneys, ureters - urinary system
    Adrenals - to fight infection and build muscle tone
    Thoracic (10-12), lumbar - for nerve supply

Deafness

    Direct reflex: Ear reflex

    Helper areas: Cervicals - for nerve supply
    Neck - for circulation to the area
    All toes (esp. 2-3) - for fine tuning the ears

Diabetes

    Direct reflex: Pancreas - controls blood sugar

    Helper areas: Adrenals - send hormonal message to pancreas
    Pituitary - regulates all the glands
    Liver - stores glycogen until needed

Diarrhea

    Direct reflexes: The colon - ascending and transverse colon control
    the water content

    Helper areas: Liver - to control the amount of bile
    Adrenals - for muscle tone and water balance
    Diaphragm - for tension and emotions

Diverticulitis
>	Direct reflex:	Colon - area of inflammation
>	Helper areas:	Liver/gallbladder - for lubrication
>	Adrenals - to fight infection
>	Lumbar/sacral area - for nerve supply
>	Diaphragm - for tension and emotions

Dizziness	See Vertigo

Drug Addiction
>	Helper areas:	All glands - to balance the body chemistry
>	Diaphragm - to relax stress and tension
>	Liver, kidneys - to detoxify

Dry Skin
>	Helper areas:	Thyroid - secretes hormone essential to normal
>	growth and development of tissue
>	Adrenals - to regulate water content of the body

Ear Infection
>	Direct reflex:	Ear reflex
>	Helper areas:	All toes - for fine tuning the ears
>	Cervicals (1-2) - for nerve supply
>	Neck/Throat - for blood supply and eustachian tube
>	Adrenals - to fight infection

Eczema
>	Helper areas:	All glands esp. adrenals, thyroid - the glands for
>	skin conditions and to balance body chemistry
>	Liver, kidneys - to detoxify
>	Intestines - for food allergies
>	Diaphragm - to relax nerves and tension

Edema
>	Helper areas:	Adrenals - for the water balance
>	Lymphatics - to move fluid out of tissue spaces
>	Kidneys - to remove excess fluid
>	Pituitary - Stimulates adrenals and the kidneys

Emphysema
    Direct reflex: Chest/lung - area affected
    Helper areas: Adrenals - for the adrenaline which relaxes muscles
                              for easier breathing
                          Diaphragm - to relax nerves and tension
                          Ileocecal - to control the mucus
                          Kidneys - for fluid retention
                          Lymphatics - to remove excess fluids

Encephalitis
    Direct reflex: Great toes - for the brain
    Helper areas: Small toes - for fine tuning the brain
                          Adrenal - for the inflammation
                          All glands - to balance the body chemistry

Epilepsy
    Helper areas: Great toe and small toes - for the brain
                          Cervicals - for nerve supply
                          Neck - to relax muscles and for blood supply
                          All glands - epilepsy can be an endocrine disorder
                          Diaphragm - to relax nervous tension

Eye Conditions
    Direct reflex: Eye reflex
    Helper areas: Small toes (2-3) - for fine tuning the eyes
                          Cervicals - for nerve supply
                          Neck - for blood supply
                          Kidneys - they can have an affect on the eyes

Fainting
    Helper area: Pituitary - as the master gland

Fatigue (general)
    Helper areas: Adrenals - for our "giddy-up-and-go"
                          Pituitary - as the master gland
                          Thyroid - to regulate metabolism
                          Whole spine - for nerve supply
                          Diaphragm - to relax nervous tension

Feet (cold and sweaty)
    Helper areas: All glands (esp. thyroid) - for hormone balance
                             Liver, intestines, kidneys - to detoxify
                             Lumbar/sacral - for nerve supply

Fever
    Helper area: Pituitary - as the master gland

Flatulence
    Helper areas: Sigmoid colon, Intestines, stomach - for the
                             formation of gas
                             Liver/gallbladder - for better digestion
                             Pancreas - for digestion

Fluid Retention   See Edema

Fracture
    Direct reflex: Reflex to affected area on foot
    Helper areas: Parathyroid - for the calcium
                             Diaphragm - to relax stress and pain
    Referral area: Referral area to affected area

Gall Stones
    Direct reflex: Gallbladder
    Helper areas: Liver , thyroid - for the cholesterol level

Gas Pains
    Helper areas: Sigmoid colon - often the start of gas pain
                             Stomach, intestines, liver, pancreas - for better
                             digestion
                             Diaphragm - for the emotions

Glandular Fever   See Mononucleosis

Glaucoma
    Direct reflex: Eye reflex
    Helper areas: Cervicals - for nerve supply
                          Neck - for blood supply
                          Small toes (2-3) - for fine tuning the eyes
                          Kidneys - they have an affect on the eyes

Gout
    Direct reflex: Reflex to affected area
    Helper area: Kidneys - for the uric acid
                          Adrenals - for inflammation

Grave's Disease - An autoimmune disease
    Direct reflex: Thyroid - to balance secretion of thyroid hormones
    Helper areas: Pituitary - TSH hormone sends message to thyroid
                          Adrenals - for corticosteroid as an anti-inflammatory

Growths (abnormal)
    Helper areas: Pituitary - for abnormal growth
                          Reflex to affected area

Hardening of the Arteries -   See Arteriosclerosis

Hay Fever
    Helper areas: All toes - for sinuses
                          Chest/lung - to improve breathing
                          All glands - to balance body and help immunity
                             esp. adrenal - infection or inflammation
                        Ileocecal - for mucus
                        Diaphragm - relax nerves and tension

Halitosis (bad breath)
    Direct reflex: All toes - represent everything in the head
    Helper areas: Digestive system (esp. stomach, liver, intestines) -
                             for better digestion

Headache (general)
Direct reflex: All toes
Helper areas: Whole spine - one end affects the other end
Diaphragm - to relax tension
All glands - to balance body chemistry

Heartburn
Helper areas: Esophagus - acid backs up from stomach
Stomach, pancreas - for digestive juices
Gallbladder - for the digestion of fats
Diaphragm - to relax stress and tension

Heart Conditions
Direct reflex: Chest/lung - for the heart
Helper areas: Diaphragm - to relax stress and tension
Cervicals, thoracics - for nerve supply to heart
Adrenal - adrenaline stimulates the heart
Parathyroid - for normal muscle function
Sigmoid - gas builds up in this area of colon

Hemorrhoids
Direct reflex: Rectum
Helper areas: Sigmoid - for congestion in this area of colon
Adrenals - for muscle tone
Liver - for lubrication
Lumbar/sacral/coccyx - for nerve supply and pressure in area
Diaphragm - to reduce stress and tension
Chronic area up the back of the leg

Hernia (Inguinal)
Direct reflex: Groin reflex
Helper areas: Intestines - for weakness in the walls
Adrenals - for muscle tone

Hiatus Hernia
    Direct reflex: Diaphragm
    Helper areas: Esophagus - ruptures or loses muscle tone
                             Stomach - acid from stomach can inflame
                                esophagus
                             Adrenals - for the muscle tone and inflammation

Hiccoughs
    Helper areas: Diaphragm - to help breathing
                             Stomach - esophagus - for the formation of gas

High Blood Pressure   (Hypertension)
    Helper areas: Diaphragm - to relax nervous system
                             Kidneys - as a diuretic, to remove excess fluid
                             Pituitary, adrenal, thyroid - for hormone balance

High Cholesterol
    Helper areas: Thyroid - sends message to liver
                             Liver - controls cholesterol

Hip (pain)
    Direct reflex: Hip/sciatic
    Helper areas: Pelvic area, knee/leg - for nerve, blood supply
                             Lumbar/sacral - for nerve supply
                             Shoulder - same zone, one of four corners of torso
    Referral area: Shoulder

Hot Flashes
    Direct reflex: Reproductive system
    Helper areas: All glands - for hormone balance
                                 esp. adrenal - for estrogen secretion
                                 thyroid - considered third ovary
                             Chronic uterus area up the back of the leg
                             Diaphragm - for the emotions

Hyperactivity
    Helper areas: Diaphragm - to relax nervous system
                             All glands - to balance body chemistry
                             Adrenal - to slow down secretion of adrenaline

Hypertension   See High Blood Pressure

Hypoglycemia
    Direct reflex: Pancreas - to balance blood sugar
    Helper areas: Liver - helps maintain blood glucose level
                            Pituitary - as the master gland
                            Adrenals - tell pancreas when to work

Hypotension
    Helper areas: Adrenals - for muscle tone of the arteries
                            Pituitary - as the master gland
                            Thyroid - it helps the other glands

Hysterectomy
    Direct reflexes: Uterus, ovaries, and fallopian (uterine) tubes
    Helper areas: Pituitary - as the master gland
                            Adrenals - secrete the hormone, estrogen
                            Thyroid - it is considered the third ovary
                            Chronic uterus area up the back of the leg
                            Diaphragm - to relax stress and tension

Impotence
    Direct reflexes: Testes and prostate
    Helper areas: All glands - the glands support each other
                            Lumbar/sacral - for nerve supply
                            Diaphragm - to relax stress and tension

Incontinence
    Direct reflex: Bladder
    Helper areas: Kidneys, ureters - the urinary system
                            Adrenals - for muscle tone
                            Lumbar/sacral - for nerve supply

Indigestion
    Helper areas: Stomach - for gastric juices
                            Liver/gallbladder, pancreas- for digestive juices
                            Sigmoid - for the formation of gas in the colon
                            Intestines - for absorption and digestion of nutrients
                            Diaphragm - to relax the nerves

Infections
    Direct reflex: Region or area affected
    Helper areas: Adrenals - to fight infection
                         Lymphatics - to carry away impurities
                         Spleen - infection (white cells)
                         Liver, kidneys - to detoxify

Infertility
    Direct reflex: Gonads/reproductive system
    Helper areas: All glands - to balance hormones
                         Lumbar/sacral - for nerve supply
                         Diaphragm - to relax tension

Influenza
    Helper areas: Chest/lung - for congestion
                         Pituitary - for fever reduction
                         All glands - to balance body chemistry
                         Lymphatics - to help clean the body
                         Ileocecal - for mucus
                         Diaphragm - to relax stress and tension

Insomnia
    Helper areas: Diaphragm - to relax stress and tension
                         All glands - to balance body chemistry
                         Pineal - it secrets melatonin which promotes sleep

Jaundice
    Direct reflex: Liver/gallbladder
    Helper area: Thoracics (4 - 9) - for nerve supply
                         Adrenal, thyroid - to calm the skin

Kidney Stones
    Direct reflex;   Kidneys
    Helper areas: Ureters, bladder - to help pass stones
                         Parathyroid - controls calcium balance
                         Diaphragm - to help control discomfort
                         Adrenals - for muscle tone

Knee Problems
        Direct reflex: Knee/leg
        Helper areas;   Hip/sciatic - for nerve and blood supply
                              Pelvic region - for nerve and blood supply
                              Lumbar/sacral - for nerve supply
        Referral area: Elbow

Laryngitis
        Direct reflex: Throat/neck
        Helper areas: All toes - for the zone breakdown of the head
                              Chest/lung - for the congestion
                              Diaphragm - to relax tension
                              Adrenals - for inflammation
                              Lymphatic system - adenoids and tonsils may
                                 be affected

Leg Aches
        Direct reflex: Knee/leg
        Helper area: Lumbar/sacral - for nerve supply
                              Groin reflex - for circulation down the leg
                              Hip/sciatic, pelvic area - for nerve, blood supply
        Referral area: Arm

Legs (swelling)
        Direct reflex: Knee/leg
        Helper areas: Kidneys - for fluid balance
                              Adrenals - for balance of sodium
                              Lymphatics - fluid elimination from tissue spaces

Leukemia
        Helper areas: Spleen - is one of the main filters for the blood
                              Lymphatics - to remove foreign cells
                              Liver - to detoxify the blood
                              All glands - for chemistry of bloodstream

Liver Conditions
        Direct reflexes: Liver/gallbladder
        Helper area: Thoracic (4 - 9) - for nerve supply

Lou Gehrig's Disease - See Amyotrophic Lateral Sclerosis

Low Blood Pressure - See Hypotension

Lupus (systemic)   An inflammatory disease
    Helper areas: All glands - to balance body chemistry
                            Intestines - for digestion
                            Liver - to detoxify
                            Whole spine - for nerve supply
                            Diaphragm - for nerve supply

Meningitis
    Direct reflex: All toes - especially for the brain
    Helper areas: Whole spine - for nerve supply
                            All glands - to balance body chemistry

Menstrual Cramps   See Cramps (menstrual)

Migraine
    Direct reflex: All toes - for the head
    Helper areas: Pituitary - as the master gland
                            Whole spine (esp. cervicals, lower spine) -
                                one end of spine affects the other end
                            Neck - for tense muscles
                            Liver - cleanse toxins
                            Diaphragm - to relax tension
                            Intestines - for digestion

Mononucleosis (infectious) or Glandular Fever
    Helper areas: Lymphatics/spleen - for enlarged lymph nodes
                            All glands - to balance body chemistry
                            Whole spine - for central nervous system
                            Diaphragm - for nervous system

Morning Sickness
    Direct reflex: All glands
    Helper areas: Diaphragm - to relax nervous system
                            Stomach - to normalize digestive secretions

Motion Sickness (land, sea, air)
    Direct reflex: Ear reflex (Inner ear) - for the equilibrium
    Helper areas: Neck - to relax muscles, and for blood supply
                      Cervicals - for nerve supply
                      Diaphragm - to relax nerves
                      Stomach - for nausea

Mucus
    Direct reflex: Ileocecal - controls mucus
    Helper areas: Chest/lung - for the congestion
                      All toes - for sinuses
                      Adrenals - for inflammation

Multiple Sclerosis
    Helper areas: Whole spine - for nervous system
                      All glands - to balance body chemistry
                      Great toes - especially for the brain
                      Diaphragm - to relax nerves

Myasthenia Gravis   An autoimmune disease
    Helper areas: Parathyroids - for smooth function of muscles
                      Adrenals - for steroids as an immunosuppressive
                      Tip of great toes - for the brain
                      Whole spine, neck - for central nervous system
                      Chest/lung - for the ease of breathing
                      Diaphragm - for sympathetic nervous system

Nausea
    Helper areas: Liver/gall bladder - for digestion
                      Stomach - for digestion
                      Diaphragm - to relax nervous tension

Neck Aches
    Direct reflex: Neck
    Helper areas: Cervicals - for nerve supply
                      Low back - one end of spine affects the other end
                      Shoulders - for nerve and blood supply

Nephritis
	Direct reflex:	Kidneys - for the nephrons
	Helper area:	Ureter tubes, bladder - part of system
			Adrenals - for inflammation of the nephrons
			Lower spine - nerve supply

Nervousness
	Helper areas:	Diaphragm - to relax stress and tension
			All glands (esp. thyroid) - to balance body chemistry
			Whole spine - for nervous system

Neuritis
	Direct reflex:	Reflex area to affected region
	Helper areas:	Whole spine - for central nervous system
			Diaphragm - to relax nerves
			All glands - for hormone balance

Ovarian Cysts
	Direct reflex:	Ovaries
	Helper areas:	Uterus, fallopian (uterine) tubes - the reproductive
				system
			Pituitary - controls the growth of foreign cells
			All glands - the glands support each other

Paralysis
	Direct reflex:	Reflex to affected area
	Helper areas:	All toes - especially for the brain
			Whole spine - for nerve supply

Parkinson's Disease
	Helper areas:	All toes - especially for the brain
			Whole spine - for central nervous system
			All glands - to balance body chemistry
				esp. adrenals - for muscle tone
			Diaphragm - to relax nerves

Perspiring Hands and Feet
     Helper areas: All glands (esp. thyroid) - for hormone balance
                                 Liver - to detoxify
                                 Kidneys - to filter waste products
                                 Intestines - to detoxify
                                 Diaphragm - to relax stress and tension

Phlebitis
     Helper areas: Adrenals - for muscle tone and inflammation
                                 Colon - constipation causes pressure on abdominal
                                   area, cutting off circulation in legs
                                 Liver/gallbladder - for bile to lubricate colon
     Referral area: Arm

Pink Eye   See Conjunctivitis

Pleurisy
     Direct reflex: Chest/lung - area affected
     Helper areas: Lymphatics - fight infection and drainage
                                 Adrenals - to reduce inflammation in pleura
                                 Diaphragm - to help lungs relax

Pneumonia
     Direct reflex: Chest/lung - area affected
     Helper areas: Diaphragm - to help relax the lungs
                                 All glands esp.
                                     adrenals - for infection
                                     pituitary - for fever
                               Ileocecal - for the mucus
                               Lymphatics - to clear up infection

Pregnancy
     Direct reflexes: Uterus, ovaries, fallopian (uterine) tubes - the
                                 reproductive system
     Helper areas: All glands - for hormone balance
                                 Whole spine - for nerve supply
                                 Bladder - fetus puts pressure on bladder
                                 Diaphragm - to relax stress and tension

Premenstrual Syndrome (PMS)
    Helper areas: Ovaries - estrogen-progesterone balance
                                    Pituitary - for antidiuretic hormone
                                    Thyroid - as third ovary and body metabolism
                                    Adrenals - helps with estrogen
                                    Kidneys, lymphatics - for release of fluid build-up
                                    Diaphragm - for the emotions

Prostate Problems
    Direct reflex: Prostate
    Helper areas: Testes, groin area - the reproductive system
                                    Pituitary - for foreign growth
                                    Adrenal - for the sex hormones
                                    Bladder - to help urination
                                    Lumbar/sacral - for nerve supply
                                    Chronic prostate area up back of leg

Psoriasis
    Helper areas: All glands (esp. thyroid and adrenals) - to help skin
                                            conditions
                                    Liver, kidneys - to detoxify
                                    Intestines - for cleansing
                                    Diaphragm - to relax stress and tension

Pyorrhea
    Helper areas: Great toes and small toes - for the teeth and gums
                                    All glands - to help fight infection and balance body
                                    chemistry

Restless Leg Syndrome
    Direct reflex: Knee/leg
    Helper areas: Lumbar - for nerve supply
                                      Hip/sciatic, pelvic area - for nerve, blood supply
                                    Shoulder - to balance four corners of the torso

Ruptured Disk
    Direct reflex: Reflex to affected area of spine
    Helper area: Diaphragm - to relax the pain

Sciatica
    Direct reflex: Hip/sciatic
    Helper areas: Knee/leg, pelvic area - for nerve, blood supply
                     Lumbar/sacral - origin of the nerve supply
                     Chronic sciatic area up back of leg
                     Shoulder - to balance four corners of the torso
    Referral area: Shoulder

Scoliosis
    Direct reflex: Whole spine
    Helper areas: Chest/lung - for pressure caused on this area
                     Shoulder - stress from curvature
                     All glands - to balance body chemistry

Shingles
    Helper areas: Whole spine - for nerve supply
                     All glands (esp. adrenals) - to fight infection
                     Diaphragm/solar plexus - for pain, to relax nerves

Shoulder Pain
    Direct reflex: Shoulder (top and bottom)
    Helper areas: Cervicals/upper thoracics - for nerve supply
                     Neck - for nerve and blood circulation
                     Hip/sciatic - to balance four corners of the torso
                     Diaphragm - for pain
    Referral area: Hip

Sinusitis
    Direct reflex: Small toes
    Helper areas: Great toes - represents everything in the head
                     Chest/lung - for the mucus in lungs
                     Ileocecal - to control the mucus
                     Adrenals - to fight infection

Smell
    Helper areas: Great toes - represent everything in the head
                     Small toes - for fine tuning for head

Sore Throat
    Direct reflex: Neck/throat
    Helper areas: Small toes - for sinus drainage
                          Cervicals - for nerve supply
                          Lymphatics - for tonsils and infection
                          Adrenals - for inflammation

Sprain or Strain
    Direct reflex: Reflex area on hand or foot corresponding to sprain
    Referral area: Referral area to affected area

Spur on Heel
    Direct reflex: Work all around the heel and then directly on spur
                          Do ankle rotation, under and over, relaxation
                             techniques

Stroke
    Direct reflex: Tip of great toe (opposite side from paralysis)
    Helper areas: Small toes - for fine tuning the head
                          Reflexes to affected areas

Sty
    Direct reflex: Eye reflex
    Helper areas: Small toes (2-3) - same zone for fine tuning
                          Cervicals, neck - for nerve and blood supply
                          Adrenals - to fight infection

Swelling   See Edema

Taste
    Direct reflex: Middle 1/3 of great toes
    Helper area: Small toes - for fine tuning

Teeth and Gums
    Direct reflex: Middle 1/3 of great toes
    Helper areas: Small toes - for fine tuning all zones
                          Cervicals - for nerve supply
                          Neck - for nerve and blood supply

Tension	See Nervousness

Thyroid Problems
Direct reflex: Thyroid
Helper areas: Pituitary - as the master gland
Adrenals - glands support each other

Tic douloureux
Helper areas: Neck - for nerve and blood supply
Cervicals - for nerve supply to face
Parathyroids - normalizes nerve function
Diaphragm - to relax pain

Tinnitus
Direct reflex: Inner ear reflex - for ringing in the ear
Helper areas: Cervicals - for nerve supply
Neck - for nerve and blood supply
Small toes (2-3) - same zone for fine tuning
Great toes - for everything in the head

Tonsillitis
Helper areas: Great toes, small toes - for the throat
Lymphatics - tonsils are part of lymphatic system
Adrenals - to fight infection
Cervicals, neck - for nerve supply

Toothache   See Teeth and Gums

Tremors
Helper areas: Brain/all toes - part of central nervous system
Whole spine - for nerve supply
Diaphragm/solar plexus - to relax nervous tension

Tumors
Direct: Reflex pertaining to location of tumor
Helper areas: Pituitary - controls abnormal growth
All glands - they work together for chemistry of
body

Ulcers
    Direct reflexes: Stomach or duodenum
    Helper area: Diaphragm/solar plexus - to relax nervous tension
                         Adrenals - to fight stress

Urinary Trouble
    Direct reflexes: Kidneys, ureters, bladder
    Helper areas: Adrenals - to fight infection
                         Thoracic (10-12), lumbar - for nerve supply

Varicose Veins   See Phlebitis

Vertigo
    Direct reflex;   Inner ear reflex - for balance
    Helper areas: Cervicals - for nerve supply
                         Neck - for blood supply
                         All toes (esp. 2 and 3) - same zone for fine tuning

Vitality (low)
    Helper areas: All glands (esp. adrenals/thyroid) - for hormone
                             balance
                         Whole spine - for nerve supply
                         Diaphragm/solar plexus - to relax nervous tension

Whiplash
    Helper areas: Top and bottom of foot between great toe and
                             second toe in metatarsal area - for muscles,
                             ligaments, and tendons
                         Whole spine
                             esp. Cervicals, upper thoracics - for the vertebrae
                             that have been pulled out of alignment
                             Lower spine - one end of spine effects the other

Wrist (sprain or break)
    Helper areas: Cervical (6-7), thoracic (1) - for nerve supply
                         Shoulder - for nerve and blood supply
    Referral area: Ankle

Anatomy Quiz

1. The smooth operation of all body parts are under the joint control of

   _________________________ and _________________________

2. The heart, blood, and blood vessels constitute the _____________
   system.

3. The air passageways and the lungs are included in the ___________
   system.

4. Metabolic waste disposal is mainly the job of the _______________
   system.

5. The spleen and thymus are included in _________________ system.

6. What organ detoxifies the body? _______________________________

7. The automatic tendency to maintain a relatively constant internal

   environment is called _______________________

8. An abnormal growth of tissue is called a neoplasm or tumor.
   True or False.

9. The vertebral column is posterior to the liver.   True or False

10. The head, neck, and trunk make up the appendicular portion of the
    body.   True or False

11. The thorax, abdomen, and pelvis constitute the torso.
    True or False

12. The term tarsal refers to ankle bones.   True or False

13. The uterus and large intestine are located in the pelvic cavity.
    True or False

14. For sciatic problems it is necessary to work the sacral/coccyx
reflex.   True or False

15. Who said "Look to the spine for the cause of disease"?

    ____

16. ___________________ are the reinforcement for Reflexology that

    allow us to work one part of the body to help another part.

17. ___________________ are additional reflex areas worked to aid the
    specific region of congestion.

18. What are the 3 things that Reflexology does?___________________

    ___________________ and ___________________

19. Reflexologist do not ___________________ , ___________________ ,

    or ___________________________________

20. Give 3 helper areas for Diabetes ___________ , ___________

    and ___________________

21. Name 3 helper areas for hypotension ___________ , ___________

    and ___________________

22. Give 3 helper areas for edema ___________ , ___________

    and ___________________

23. What is the referral area for the shoulder? ___________________

24. What is the referral area for the elbow?___________________

CHAPTER QUIZ ANSWERS

Chapter One - page 11

(1) cervicals, thoracics, lumbar, sacral, coccyx   (2) 26   (3) 31, 12
(4) 26, 27   (5) axial
(6) skeletal or voluntary, smooth or involuntary, cardiac
 (7) diaphragm   (8) muscle   (9) nervous   (10) ligaments
(11) tendons   (12) 14   (13) 5   (14) discs

Chapter Two - page 16

(1) right atrium, right ventricle, left atrium, left ventricle
(2) systole, diastole   (3) pulmonary   (4) carbon dioxide, oxygen
(5) arterial   (6) oxygen, carbon dioxide   (7) electrocardiograph
(8) fat or cholesterol   (9) exercise   (10) increase

Chapter Three - page 21

(1) lymph vessels, lymph nodes, lymph tissues   (2) spleen, thymus
(3) venous   (4) muscles, exercise   (5) thymus   (6) spleen
(7) cup-shaped valves   (8) tonsils   (9) adenoids   (10) leukemia
(11) lymphatics

Chapter Four - page 27

(1) protection, temperature control, production vitamin D   (2) dermis
(3) dermis, epidermis   (4) epidermis   (5) sebum   (6) 2nd cranial
(7) cornea   (8) pupil   (9) external, middle, inner
(10) hearing, balance   (11) warms, cleans, moisturizes   (12) cilia
(13) smell   (14) taste, speech, swallowing

Chapter Five - page 32

(1) respiration   (2) costal, diaphragmatic   (3) diaphragm, intercostal
(4) paranasal sinuses, mucus   (5) pharynx   (6) larynx
(7) wind pipe   (8) larynx   (9) thoracic cavity
(10) superior, middle, inferior   (11) capillaries, oxygen, alveoli
(12) cilia   (13) pleura   (14) bronchi

Chapter Six - page 42

(1) energy, growth, repair   (2) bile   (3) mouth, saliva   (4) ptyalin
(5) liver   (6) gastrin, pepsin, hydrochloric acid
(7) duodenum, jejunum, ileum   (8) ileocecal valve   (9) liver
(10) small intestine   (11) hepatic, splenic, sigmoid
(12) gall bladder   (13) pancreas   (14) insulin, glucagon

Chapter Seven - page 46

(1) reddish-brown, bean   (2) nephrons
(3) skin, lungs, large colon, urinary system   (4) bladder   (5) kidneys
(6) hypothalamus, pituitary, kidneys   (7) arthritis   (8) ureter
(9) kidneys   (10) sphincter   (11) sodium, potassium
(12) urea, uric acid   (13) urethra   (14) anterior to (in front of)

Chapter Eight - page 56

(1) hormones, "I stimulate"   (2) parathyroid   (3) endocrine gland
(4) pituitary   (5) pancreas, glucagon   (6) hypothalamus
(7) gonadotrophin, pituitary   (8) pineal   (9) thyroid   (10) adrenal
(11) type 1 or childhood, type 2 or adult   (12) islets of Langerhans

Chapter Nine - page 63

(1) breasts   (2) prostate   (3) cryptorchidism   (4) testosterone
(5) estrogen, progesterone   (6) uterine tubes   (7) cervix
(8) menstruation   (9) ovaries, testes   (10) spermatozoa, ova
(11) scrotum   (12) bulbourethral or Cowper's glands

Anatomy Quiz - page 90

(1) endocrine glands, central nervous system   (2) cardiovascular
(3) respiratory   (4) urinary   (5) lymphatic   (6) liver
(7) homeostasis   (8) true   (9) true   (10) false   (11) true
(12) true   (13) true   (14) false   (15) Hippocrates
(16) referral areas   (17) helper areas
(18) relieve stress and tension, improve nerve and blood supply, help nature
achieve homeostasis

(19) diagnose, prescribe, treat for a specific condition
(20) liver, adrenals, pituitary   (21) adrenals, pituitary, thyroid
(22) lymphatics, kidneys, adrenals   (23) hip   (24) knee

FOOT NOTES